PC DOS: Using the IBM PC Operating System

The Wiley IBM PC Series
Laurence Press, Series Editor

*Communications on the IBM PC, Schwaderer
CP/M® for the IBM: Using CP/M-86®, Fernandez & Ashley
*IBM PC Applications Book, Press
IBM PC: Data File Programming, Brown & Finkel
*Management Science on the IBM PC, Hesse
PC DOS: Using the IBM PC Operating System, Ashley & Fernandez
PC Graphics: Charts, Graphs, Games, & Art on the IBM PC, Conklin
*What If...: A Guide to Using Electronic Work Sheets on the IBM PC,
    Williams
*Word Processing on the IBM PC, Hewes

*Forthcoming

CP/M® and CP/M-86® are registered trademarks of Digital Research.

PC DOS: Using the IBM PC Operating System

Ruth Ashley
Judi N. Fernandez
Co-Presidents
DuoTech

Wiley IBM PC Series: Series Editor, Laurence Press, Ph.D.

A Wiley Press Book
JOHN WILEY & SONS, INC.
New York · Chichester · Brisbane · Toronto · Singapore

Publisher: Judy V. Wilson
Editor: Dianne Littwin
Managing Editor: Maria Colligan
Composition and Make-up: Cobb/Dunlop, Inc.

Library of Congress Cataloging in Publication Data

Ashley, Ruth.
    PC DOS, using the IBM PC.

    (Wiley IBM PC series) (Wiley self-teaching guides)
    Includes index.
    1. IBM Personal Computer—Programming.   I. Fernandez,
Judi N., 1941–   II. Title.   III. Title: P.C.
    D.O.S., using the I.B.M. PC.   IV. Series.
QA76.8.I2594A83   1983   001.64'25   82-24720
ISBN 0-471-89718-3

Printed in the United States of America

83 84 85 10 9 8 7 6 5 4 3 2 1

Acknowledgments

We would like to thank the following people for helping in the development of this book:

Student readers:

  Paul Ashley
  Dorothy Hoogterp
  Bob Sansom
  Donna Tabler

Typists:

  Patricia Adams-Manson
  Barbara Tabler

To the Reader

DOS—the Disk Operating System—is an operating system for the IBM Personal Computer. An operating system is a set of programs that helps you operate the computer and perform routine work functions. The DOS system includes programs that allow you to run other programs, create files, erase files, copy files, print data from files, display the directory of a disk, and so on. Without DOS or a similar operating system, it would be very difficult and tedious for you to perform even the most trivial task on your computer.

This book assumes that you have an IBM Personal Computer and a DOS package. Our intent is not to help you select a system, but to help you use what you already have. If you do not yet have your system, but have selected the machine and DOS, you will still benefit from studying this book. You will need to skip the machine exercises and come back to them when your system has been set up.

There may be newer versions of DOS released in the future. Each new release is an upgrade of earlier releases. Nothing is lost, but some features may be changed or new features added. This book is current with release 1.1. However, we will warn you of differences from earlier versions.

How to Use This Book

This Self-Teaching Guide consists of 11 chapters that have been carefully sequenced to introduce you to your IBM Personal Computer and its operating system and help you develop a useful set of skills. We have made every effort to organize the material in the best possible learning sequence, so that you can begin using your machine as quickly as possible. We strongly recommend that you study the chapters in order. You will learn to do easy tasks, then successively more complex tasks, until you have mastered the system.

Each chapter begins with a short introduction followed by objectives, which outline what you can expect to learn from it, and ends with a Self-Test, which allows you to measure your learning and practice what you have studied. Each chapter also contains a Suggested Machine Exercise that guides you in transferring your new knowledge to the real, hands-on environment.

The body of each chapter is divided into frames—short numbered sections in which information is presented or reviewed, followed by questions that ask you to apply the information. The correct answers to these questions follow a dashed line after the frame. As you work through the book, use a folded paper or a card to cover the correct answer until you have written yours. Be sure you actually write each response, especially when the activity is coding commands. Only by writing out the commands, and checking them carefully, can you get the most from this Self-Teaching Guide.

And don't worry! There's almost nothing you can do, apart from outright physical abuse, that can damage your system. Certainly there's no command you can enter that will hurt either PC DOS or the hardware. At the most, you can lose some data, and that's what this book and the Suggested Machine Exercises will help to prevent.

For the proper physical care of your equipment, see your manufacturer's recommendations.

Contents

PC DOS: Using the IBM PC Operating System

CHAPTER ONE

Introduction to DOS

The Disk Operating System (DOS) is a set of programs that runs the IBM Personal Computer. To be more specific, DOS enables you to control the operation of the microcomputer.

In this first chapter we talk about the Personal Computer itself—the pieces of equipment that are required and optional when you're going to use DOS. You will also learn how to start the computer with DOS and handle any problems you might encounter.

When you have finished this chapter, you will be able to:

- Identify the major components of the Personal Computer
- Start up DOS
- Interpret error messages that may result from starting up DOS

PERSONAL COMPUTER COMPONENTS

The Personal Computer includes a system unit containing memory and at least one disk drive, a keyboard, a color or monochrome monitor, and perhaps some other equipment as well. We'll look at these components before we talk about how to start up the computer.

1. The heart of the Personal Computer is contained in the *system unit*. Inside this unit is the microprocessor, which is the component containing the computer's logic and arithmetic circuits. It is the microprocessor that reads and executes programs. The system unit also contains memory—a set of circuits for storing programs and data while the microprocessor is working on them.

One or two disk drives are built into the system unit. Our picture shows two disk drives, but your computer may have only one. The disk drives are used for storing programs and data so that the computer can copy them into memory when needed.

System Unit

(a) Name three components inside the system unit. _____

_____

(b) Which component does the arithmetic and logic work?_____

_____

(c) Which component stores the programs and data that the computer might

want to copy?_____

(d) Which component stores the programs and data that the computer is cur-

rently using?_____

_ _ _ _ _ _ _ _ _ _ _

(a) microprocessor, memory, disk drives; (b) microprocessor; (c) disk drives; (d)
memory

2.   The IBM personal computer may have from 16K to 1024K (also called 1M) of
memory. For any program to run on your computer, it must be stored in memory.
(This includes the DOS programs.)

In computer terms, "K" refers to about one thousand—actually 1024—and so
16K means 16,384 bytes. A *byte* is the amount of storage space required to store
one character of data. "M" refers to about one million—1,048,576 bytes. Therefore a Personal Computer may hold anywhere from 16,384 to 1,048,576 characters of data, depending on how much memory it has.

(a) What term refers to the amount of storage needed to store one letter, such as

"B"?_____

(b)   How would you specify that memory has room for about 32,000 characters?

_____

— — — — — — — — — — —

(a) byte; (b) 32K bytes

3.   An IBM Personal Computer that uses DOS has one or more *disk drives*. The drives use a 5¼-inch diameter "mini-floppy" disk. Each mini-floppy can hold up to 160K bytes of data on one side.

The mini-floppies are used for external storage of data. A vast amount of data can be stored this way because you can use numerous disks. They can be removed from the machine, when not in use, and other disks installed in their place. Thus, although each side holds only 160K, you may have stored millions of bytes of data on disk. The Personal Computer may have one or two disk drives and each disk drive may be capable of reading one or two sides of a disk. Thus, the computer may have access to 160K to 640K bytes of disk data at one time.

(a)   Are disk drives used for memory or external storage?_____

(b)   How many bytes does one two-sided disk hold?_____

(c)   Which is true?

_____ A.   One computer system can have only two disks, and so the maximum amount of external storage is 640K bytes.

_____ B.   Only two disks at a time may be used, but a system may have hundreds of interchangeable disks.

— — — — — — — — — — —

(a) external storage; (b) 320K; (c) B

4.   The disk drives have alphabetical names within the DOS system. The first, or only, drive is called A. If your computer has two disk drives, drive A is on the left as you face the system unit, and drive B is on the right. If you have more than two drives, the extra ones could be in a separate unit.

In the drawing below, label the disk drives with their names.

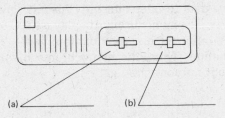

(a)_____   (b)_____

_ _ _ _ _ _ _ _ _ _

(a) A; (b) B

5. Attached to the system unit is a keyboard unit. This is the main means by which you communicate with the computer. You type commands on the keyboard, and DOS reads and obeys the commands.

Keyboard

Match these components with their functions:

___ (a)   Disk unit

___ (b)   Keyboard

___ (c)   Memory

1.   Stores programs and data currently being worked on
2.   Stores other programs and data
3.   Used to give commands to the computer

_ _ _ _ _ _ _ _ _ _

(a) 2; (b) 3; (c) 1

6. Your Personal Computer will have some type of monitor—a TV-like device that the computer uses to communicate with you. The standard monitor is a device that displays data in one color only (usually green) and so is called a monochrome display. The monochrome display is good for displaying character data such as letters, numbers, and punctuation marks, but it is not so good for graphics and animation. Thus, the monochrome display is usually used in business settings, but not for action games.

IBM Monochrome Display

Instead of, or in addition to, the standard monochrome display, you may install a special Color/Graphics Monitor Adapter and hook up another monitor, either color or some other type of monochrome display. The features you get (such as color graphics) depend on the monitor you select. In general, the more you pay, the more you get. (A TV set may be used, but it doesn't do as good a job as a monitor.)

Many home Personal Computers have *both* a monochrome display and a color monitor attached. Why do you suppose their owners hook up both types of devices?

_____

_____

— — — — — — — — — — —

The monochrome display is for "serious" work such as personal accounting and word processing, whereas the color TV is used for action games.

7. Your Personal Computer must have a system unit, keyboard, and at least one monitor. It might also have some of the units discussed below.

A *printer* is used to make permanent copies, on paper, of data. It saves you from having to copy data from the monitor screen by hand. If you install the right boards inside your system unit, you can attach more than one printer to your system.

Joysticks can be used with many action games.

Communications equipment allows your computer to send and receive data over telephone lines with other computers.

Specify whether each of the following is a required or an optional component.

(a) Joysticks _____

(b) Printer _____

(c) System unit _____

(d) Monitor (or TV) _____

(e) Communications equipment _____

(f) Keyboard _____

— — — — — — — — — —

(a) optional; (b) optional; (c) required; (d) required; (e) optional; (f) required

8. DOS monitors a microcomputer system made up of various pieces of equipment, which is called *hardware*. DOS itself, however, is *software*. That is, DOS consists of programs and data, not equipment. DOS is an *operating system*; it is a system of programs that allow you to operate your computer. The software provided by DOS acts as an interface between the microprocessor and you. It also acts as an interface between any two hardware devices.

Which of the following are functions or features of DOS?

_____ (a) Serves as a hardware device

_____ (b) Interfaces between pieces of hardware

_____ (c) Operating system

_____ (d) Software

— — — — — — — — — —

b, c, d

BOOTING

9. Let's assume now that you're ready to start your system. It has been set up and all the necessary cables connected. The power is off. How do you get DOS up and running?

Step 1: You must use a disk containing the DOS system. For now, you will use the original system disk that came with your computer. (It's in the binder with the DOS manual.) Later, we'll show you how to create and use other disks. Insert your system disk in drive A. To do this, open the tab that covers the center of the disk slot. Remove the disk from its paper sleeve. Don't try to remove it from the permanent paper envelope, however, and don't touch the mylar parts that show through the envelope. With the label up, push the disk slowly into the disk unit as far as it will go. Then close the tab again.

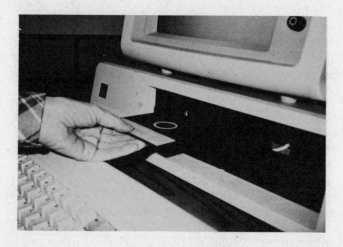

Step 2:   Turn on your printer, if you wish. On the standard IBM printer, the on/off switch is a rocker switch on the right side at the back.

Step 3:   Turn on your monitor (if it has its own power switch; the standard IBM monochrome display does not have one).

Step 4:   Turn on the main power switch on the system unit. It's on the right at the back.

Actually, steps 2 to 4 may be done in any order, but step 1 must be done before step 4.

If all goes well, DOS will *boot*. This means that the DOS system is booted (or loaded) into the computer and it begins to operate. It can take quite a while (a minute or so); so be patient.

(a)   What must you do before you turn on the main power switch?

_____

(b)   What must be on the disk you boot from?

_____ A.   BASIC

_____ B.   The DOS system

_____ C.   It must be blank

(c)   In which drive do you put the boot disk—the left-hand or right-hand one?

_____

— — — — — — — — — —

(a) put the DOS system disk in drive A; (b) B; (c) the left-hand one (if you try to boot from drive B, it won't work)

10.   A number of things can go wrong when you try to boot. For example, suppose you don't install a disk in drive A properly before turning on the power. The IBM Personal Computer BASIC system (built into the computer) will take over instead of DOS. Here's what the screen will look like:

```
The IBM Personal Computer Basic
Version C1.00 Copyright IBM Corp 1981
61404 Bytes free
Ok
```

Suppose you install a disk in drive A properly, but the disk doesn't contain the proper DOS programs. You might get one of these messages:

```
Bad or missing Command Interpreter
```

or

```
Invalid COMMAND.COM in drive A
```

or

```
Disk boot failure
```

or

```
Nonsystem disk or disk error
Replace and strike any key when ready
```

In all but the last case, you'll need to put the correct disk in drive A and reboot. (The next frame will show you how to reboot without using the main power switch.) In the last case, you can put the disk in properly and then press any key.

Sometimes, you will try to boot and nothing at all will happen. If the cursor (the little blinking line) does not appear in about 5 to 10 seconds, or if it appears but nothing else happens after a minute or so, turn the system off again. Wait a minute or two, and then try again with a different disk.

Suppose you try to boot DOS and get this message:

```
The IBM Personal Computer Basic
Version C1.00 Copyright IBM Corp 1981
61404 Bytes free
Ok
```

(a) What's wrong?_____

_____

(b) How can you fix it?_____

_____

Suppose you try to boot DOS and get this message:

Bad or missing Command Interpreter

(c) What's wrong?_____

_____

(d) How can you fix it?_____

_____

— — — — — — — — — — —

(a) you didn't put a disk in drive A properly, and so BASIC has taken over; (b) install the disk properly and reboot; (c) the disk you tried to boot from is not a good boot disk; (d) install a proper disk and reboot

11. Sometimes you want to reboot; that is, restart DOS without using the power switch. You usually do this to get rid of a bad program or command or to recover from a bad initial boot. When you reboot, DOS stops whatever it is doing and goes back to the beginning.

You don't have to shut the power off to reboot. All you have to do is make sure the system disk is in drive A and then press three keys simultaneously: Ctrl, Alt, and Del. You can hold down Ctrl and Alt with your left hand and press Del with your right hand. The process is intentionally awkward to prevent your rebooting accidentally and terminating a program you were using.

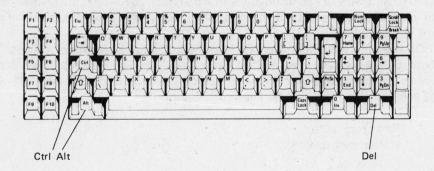

Ctrl Alt   Del

(a) Rebooting interrupts (aborts) whatever the computer is currently doing. True or false?_____

(b) What keys are used in rebooting?

_____

(c) In what order must they be pressed?

_____

— — — — — — — — — —

(a) true; (b) Ctrl, Alt, Del; (c) all together

ENTERING THE DATE

12. When the system is booted or rebooted properly, the following message is displayed:

```
Current date is Tue 1–01–1980
Enter new date:
```

This line represents the cursor, a line on your screen that flashes on and off to tell you where the next letter you type will be placed.

DOS always starts off thinking it is January 1, 1980. You should change it to the current date. DOS uses the date when it records data on a disk; so the date can be important to you. (*Note:* DOS versions earlier than 1.1 behave slightly differently when booted.)

You don't specify the day of the week; DOS figures that out from the date you enter. Dates are specified numerically, using either hyphens or slashes to separate the three parts. The month must a number from 1 through 12. The day must be a number from 1 through 31. (You may omit leading zeros.) The year can be a two-digit number from 80 through 99, in which case 1980–1999 is assumed, or a four-digit number from 1980 through 2099. DOS cannot handle dates before 1980 or after 2099.

DOS does not remember the date from boot to boot. Every time you boot or reboot, DOS goes back to its earliest date: 1–01–1980 (a Tuesday). If you don't want to use the current date, you can just hit Enter and DOS will use 1–01–80.

If you enter an invalid date, here's what happens:

```
Invalid date
Enter new date:
```

(a) Which of the following will DOS accept as legitimate dates?

_____ A. 5/10/70   _____ D. March 3, 2000   _____ G. 12–1–1982

_____ B. 6/19/81   _____ E. 3–3–03   _____ H. 12/9/1995

_____ C. 20–1–99   _____ F. 3/3/2003   _____ I. 4/6

(b) Suppose today is June 5, 1990.

Enter new date: _____

(c) Suppose today is May 10, 2001.

Enter new date: _____

(d) You can enter any old nonsense for today's date because the system doesn't use it for anything. True or false? _____

(e) You should enter the current date every time you boot or reboot because DOS always goes back to 1–01–1980. True or false? _____

———————————

(a) B, F, G, H [A—70 is not a legitimate year; C—20 is not a legitimate month; D—wrong format; E—03 is not a legitimate year, although 2003 is; I needs a year]; (b) one correct answer is 6–5–90; (c) one correct answer is 5–10–2001 (be sure you used four digits for the year); (d) false—it's used in the disk directory; (e) true—unless you want to use 1–01–1980 as the date

Note: Now you have learned how to boot DOS and how it responds. If you have a computer available, why don't you practice that much before going on. Don't bother changing the date now.

13.   Whenever you want to enter any data, such as the date, you type the data and then hit the Enter key, which looks like this:

Enter

It is in the same position that the CARRIAGE RETURN key is in on most electric typewriters, where you can hit it with the little finger of your right hand.

DOS will not read the data until you hit the Enter key.

(a)   When this book or one of your other manuals tells you to "enter" something, what two steps are involved?_____

_____

(b)   DOS reads each character as you type it. True or false?_____

(c)   What symbol is on the Enter key?_____

— — — — — — — — —

(a) type the data, hit Enter; (b) false—it waits until you press Enter; (c) ↵

ENTERING THE TIME

14.   After the date has been entered, you'll see a message similar to this:

```
Current time is 0:00:12.02
Enter new time:_
```

In the above example, 12.02 seconds have elapsed since DOS was booted. (It probably took 12.02 seconds to enter the date.) Whenever you boot or reboot, DOS resets the time to midnight (0:00:00.0).

The time is expressed in hours:minutes:seconds.hundredths. To enter a new time, you can type hours between 0 and 23, minutes and seconds between 0 and 59, and hundredths of seconds between 0 and 99. Leading zeros may be omitted. Colons must be used between hours, minutes, and seconds. A period must be used between seconds and hundredths. Any value you omit will be assumed to be zero. Thus, 10:30 means 10:30:00.00 and 5 means 5:00:00.00. 24-hour time is used, so that's five o'clock in the morning. 17:00:00.00 is five o'clock in the evening.

If the time goes past midnight during one session, the date is automatically revised.

If you enter an invalid time, you'll see this message:

```
Invalid time
Enter new time:_
```

If you don't want to enter a new time, just hit Enter and the current time will be used.

What would you type to enter the following times?

(a) Two o'clock in the afternoon. _____

(b) Three minutes and ten seconds after midnight. _____

(c) Ten minutes after nine in the morning. _____

(d) The default time (in computerese, "default" means the value that is automatically used if you don't enter a different one). _____

_ _ _ _ _ _ _ _ _ _

(a) 14 (b) 0:3:10 (c) 9:10 (d) Enter

15. After you have entered a valid time, you will see this message:

```
The IBM Personal Computer DOS
Version n.nn (C) Copyright IBM Corp. (dates)

A>_
```

This message tells you that DOS is up and running.
Put these three messages in their proper order.

_____ (a)   The IBM Personal Computer DOS

Version n.nn (C) Copyright IBM Corp. (dates)

_____ (b)   Current time is time

Enter new time:_

_____ (c)   Current date is Tue 1–01–1980

Enter new date:_

_ _ _ _ _ _ _ _ _ _

(a) 3; (b) 2; (c) 1

Note: Disks can be arranged so that the Date and Time features are bypassed and another program is invoked as part of the booting process. In such cases, the booting procedure that we've described here does not take place. What *does* happen depends on the program that is invoked. You'll learn all about this DOS feature later in this book. For now, we just want you to know that you might boot with a disk that bypasses the normal boot procedure. In any case, a new DOS system disk will boot as we described.

USING YOUR DOS MANUAL

16. If you have trouble remembering the boot procedure, you can look it up. You can come back to this book or use one of your IBM reference manuals. Both the Disk Operating System manual and the Guide to Operations manual explain how to boot.

If you encounter a message you don't understand, look it up in your DOS manual. There is an appendix showing all the DOS messages in alphabetical order. Find that appendix now and use it to answer the following question.

Suppose you're trying to print something and you get this message:

```
Printer fault
```

What does it mean?

_____ (a) The printer is broken.

_____ (b) The printer can't interpret the data being sent to it.

_____ (c) The printer is out of paper or ribbon.

_____ (d) The printer is off line (not hooked up to the computer properly).

_ _ _ _ _ _ _ _ _

d

SHUTTING THE SYSTEM DOWN

17. How do you shut the system down again? Turn off the power. You can remove the disks either before or after you shut it down. Store your disks carefully. They're not overly fragile, but they're not hardy either. They don't like dust, dirt, fingerprints, liquids, scratches, or magnets. It's best to keep them in their paper sleeves and inside another container—a box or a binder.

(a) True or false? You must remove the disks before you shut off the system

unit. _____

(b) True or false? Floppy disks need to be handled and stored carefully.

_____

_ _ _ _ _ _ _ _ _

(a) false—they can be removed either before or after the power is shut off; (b) true

Now you have learned which hardware components are required by DOS, how to start up (boot) DOS, and how to shut it down again.

Chapter One Self-Test

This Self-Test will help you determine if you have mastered the objectives of this chapter. Answer each question to the best of your ability, and then check your answers in the answer key at the end of the test.

1. Which of the following are required components of a personal computer under DOS?

    _____ a. Memory

    _____ b. Disk drive(s)

    _____ c. Tape drive(s)

    _____ d. Monitor or TV

    _____ e. Paper tape reader

    _____ f. Printer

    _____ g. Keyboard

2. Which drive do you boot from?_____ Which side is that on?_____

3. Put the following boot steps in order.

    _____ a. Turn on main power switch on system unit.

    _____ b. Put proper disk in boot drive.

    _____ c. Turn on printer and monitor.

4. Suppose you try to boot and get this message:

    `Bad or missing Command Interpreter`

    a. What's wrong?_____

    b. How can you fix it?_____

    _____

5. Which keys are used to reboot?

    _____

6. Which of the following is true?

    _____ a. DOS reads each character as you type it.

    _____ b. DOS reads data when you stop typing for more than 5 seconds.

    _____ c. DOS reads data when you press the Enter key.

7. Code the following as valid dates for DOS.

   a. January 10, 1982: _____

   b. March 16, 1999: _____

   c. August 19, 2006: _____

8. Code the following as valid times for DOS.

   a. Four o'clock in the morning: _____

   b. Thirteen minutes after seven in the evening: _____

   c. Two seconds after noon: _____

9. Which of the following is true?

   _____ a. You can use the default date or time by just pushing Enter.

   _____ b. You must enter a valid date and time whenever you boot or reboot.

Self-Test Answer Key

Compare your answers to the Self-Test with the correct answers given below. If all your answers are correct, you are ready to go on to the Suggested Machine Exercise. If you missed any questions, you may find it helpful to review the appropriate frames before going on.

1. a, b, d, g
2. A, left
3. a – 2 or 3; b – 1; c – 2 or 3
4. a. Something's wrong with the disk you're booting from.
   b. Install a good boot disk and reboot.
5. Ctrl, Alt, Del
6. c
7. a. Any of the following is correct:

1–10–82	1–10–1982
1/10/82	1/10/1982

   b. Any of the following is correct:

3–16–99	3–16–1999
3/16/99	3/16/1999

   c. Either of the following is correct:

   8–19–2006
   8/19/2006

8. a. 4
   b. 19:13
   c. 12:00:02
9. a

Suggested Machine Exercise

Each chapter in this book ends with a suggested machine exercise. If you have your Personal Computer and DOS disk, we strongly recommend that you work these exercises. This is the best way to become comfortable with DOS.

If you don't know how to boot your system, this first exercise is vital because every other exercise in this book starts by booting.

Your system must be set up before you work this exercise. That is, it must be out of the box and all the cables must be hooked up properly. If your system has not yet been set up, follow the directions in your Guide to Operations. Then work the exercise below.

1. Boot the system using your DOS system disk.
2. If you get no date message, try again. (Look up any strange messages in your DOS manual.)
3. If all else fails, get help.
4. If the boot succeeds, you should get a message like this:

   ```
   Current date is Tue 1-01-1980
   Enter new date:_
   ```

5. Enter the correct date. You should get a message like this:

   ```
   Current time is 0:00:16:25
   Enter new time:_
   ```

6. Enter the current time. You should get a message like this:

   ```
   The IBM Personal Computer DOS
   Version n.nn (C)Copyright IBM Corp. dates
   ```

7. Try rebooting. (Hold down Ctrl and Alt and press Del.)
8. Try entering an invalid date or time. Then use the default.
9. Try a few "bad" boots so you can see the messages. Try rebooting with no disk in drive A. Try rebooting with a blank disk in drive A.

Take the time now to make a backup copy of your DOS system disk. The following steps explain how. (You will study this process in detail in Chapter Seven.)

10. Reboot with the DOS system disk in drive A.
11. Use any date and time. The defaults are fine.

12. Next to "A>" type this word: diskcopy. The computer will respond:

```
Insert source diskette in drive A:
Strike any key when ready
```

13. Since you want to copy the DOS system disk, which is already in drive A, press Enter. The computer will respond:

```
Copying 1 side(s)
Insert target diskette in drive A:
Strike any key when ready
```

(You will also hear it reading from drive A.)

14. Remove the DOS disk from drive A.

15. Insert a blank disk in drive A. Be sure to use a blank disk, as any data will be erased from the disk you use. Be sure the disk has a small notch in the upper right-hand corner, like this:

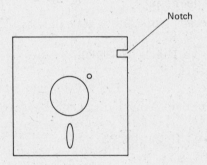

Notch

(You'll learn why later.)

16. Press Enter. You will hear the system writing on your disk. Then you will see this message:

```
Insert source diskette in drive A:
Strike any key when ready
```

If you get any other message, go back to step 15 and use a different disk.

17. Remove the second disk and reinstall the DOS system disk. Press Enter. You will soon see this message:

```
Insert target diskette in drive A:
Strike any key when ready
```

18. Remove the DOS system disk and install your copy disk.

19. Repeat steps 16 through 18 until you see this message:

```
Copy complete
Copy another (Y/N)?
```

You'll have to repeat steps 16 through 18 about three times.

20. Type the letter n. (Don't press Enter.) The system will respond with "A>".

21. You have now made a backup copy of your DOS system disk. Put the original away and use only the backup from now on. Put a label on the copy and mark it "DOS". (Don't press too hard on the disk when you write on the label or you'll damage the disk.) Shut down your system and go on to Chapter Two.

CHAPTER TWO

The DOS Components

You're seen what hardware your computer can use with DOS. Now it's time to look at the DOS software side. In this chapter, you'll learn what programs DOS includes. You'll also learn how DOS organizes and controls data on disks, and how DOS responds to your commands.

When you have finished this chapter, you will be able to:

- Identify the functions of the major parts of the DOS system
- Recognize valid file identifiers
- Select a default disk drive
- Interpret error messages that may result from drive selection

THE DOS PROGRAMS

We have said several times that DOS is a *set* of programs. In the frames that follow, we'll overview the major DOS programs.

1. The program named IBMBIO acts as an interface between other programs and the Basic Input/Output System (BIOS). BIOS is a set of functions that controls all input and output between memory and the other devices. When a program wants to write data to the printer or read data from the keyboard (for example), the program calls on BIOS to actually handle the read or write function.

BIOS is not a part of DOS. It is so basic to the function of the computer that it is permanently built into memory. A portion of memory is reserved for permanent functions and cannot be changed. This part of memory is called Read-Only Memory (ROM) because you can read it but you can't write in it. BIOS is stored in ROM.

IBMBIO provides an interface to BIOS. This interface processes other programs' requests for BIOS functions. In addition, IBMBIO identifies and prevents problems caused by dividing by zero (this is always a problem in computers), the printer running out of paper, and other situations.

(a) What do the following terms stand for?

BIOS _____

ROM _____

(b) Match.

_____ A. BIOS

_____ B. IBMBIO

a. Part of ROM
b. Part of DOS
c. Identifies when the printer runs out of paper
d. Controls I/O functions
e. Interfaces programs with I/O functions
f. Prevents division by zero

_ _ _ _ _ _ _ _ _ _

(a) Basic Input/Output System; Read-Only Memory; (b) A—a, d; B—b, c, e, f

2.   Another DOS program is called IBMDOS. It controls the organization of data on the disks.

Data is kept on disk in files. A file is a set of related data. For example, your office might have a payroll file that contains the payroll information for all your company's employees.

The file, in turn, contains records. For the payroll file there would be one record for each employee containing the employee's name, address, wage rate, tax rate, and so forth.

The payroll file is an example of a data file. Another type of file you will have is a program file, which contains all the instructions that make up one computer program. Each instruction is a record.

One disk may contain many files. It's not unusual to have more than 50 files on one disk. IBMDOS keeps track of all files on the disk.

(a) What is the basic function of IBMDOS?_____

_____

(b) Which of the following statements is true?

_____ A. A disk contains records, which contain files.

_____ B. A disk contains files, which contain records.

_ _ _ _ _ _ _ _ _ _

(a) organizes data on the disk; (b) B

3.   Every disk file must have a name. IBMDOS keeps a file *directory* on each disk. The directory shows all the file names, their sizes, and their exact locations on the disk, along with other information.

   IBMDOS also uses a File Allocation Table on each disk to show where new files can be stored.

   Every time you add a new file to a disk, IBMDOS does the following:

   - Checks the directory to make sure there is no file with the same name
   - Checks the directory to make sure there is room for the file
   - Checks the File Allocation Table to find a good location for the file
   - Updates the directory with an entry for the new file

(a)   What DOS program maintains the disk directory? _____

(b)   What information does the disk directory contain?

   _____

   _____

(c)   What is the name of the table on each disk that shows where new files can be

   put? _____

- - - - - - - - - -

(a) IBMDOS; (b) file name, file size, file location, other information; (c) File Allocation Table

4.   The preceding frames have discussed the IBMBIO and IBMDOS programs. Another major set of programs is the *command processor* (COMMAND). This is the part you will use directly. COMMAND reads whatever you type on the keyboard and processes the commands you give it. Every time you interact with DOS you use COMMAND. You can enter commands to list a directory or erase a file, and COMMAND will process the command and do as you ask. You can request processing external to COMMAND, and COMMAND will handle the request and then return to you. All your commands at the keyboard are handled through the command processor of DOS.

(a)   What is the name of the command processor? _____

(b)   Can you interact with DOS without using the command processor? _____

   If so, how? _____

- - - - - - - - - -

(a) COMMAND; (b) no

5.   The COMMAND program contains several routines for functions that you will use all the time. You will learn how to use the functions in Chapters Four and Five, but we'll overview them here:

- DIR displays the directory of a disk.
- ERASE erases a file from a disk.
- TYPE displays a file.
- RENAME renames a file.
- COPY copies one or more files.
- DATE displays and changes the internal date.
- TIME displays and changes the internal time.

Because these functions are part of the command processor, they're always available to you whenever DOS is running on your computer. The commands that you type to use them (DIR, ERASE, etc.) are called the internal commands.

(a)   What major DOS program processes the internal commands?

_____

(b)   If your computer is on but you haven't booted DOS into memory, would the internal commands work? _____ Why? _____

— — — — — — — — — —

(a) COMMAND; (b) no, because they're part of DOS

Note: If you are using a DOS version earlier than 1.1, you will have slightly different internal commands.

6.   The other DOS programs you are studying in this section, such as IBMBIO and IBMDOS, are also built into the DOS package. Whenever DOS is running on your system, they are automatically stored in memory and are available to DOS. However, you have no commands to use them. They are only called by other programs. For example, COMMAND uses IBMBIO to communicate with your keyboard.
   Even though they are internal programs, they have no matching commands.
   Match the functions below with their characteristics.

_____	(a) COMMAND, IBMBIO, IBMDOS	1. Internal commands
_____	(b) DIR, ERASE, TYPE	2. Always available when DOS is running

— — — — — — — — — —

(a) 2; (b) 1, 2

7.   Any program that is not internal is called an *external* program. The term "external" refers to the fact that the program is loaded into main memory only when it is needed. An external program is kept in a file on disk. Its filename becomes the command that you type if you want to use the program.

Your DOS system disk contains several external programs provided by IBM. You might also acquire external programs from other sources, such as a word processing program, or you might write your own.

There are only a few internal commands, but you can have as many external commands as you can fit files on your disks.

Match the program types on the left with their descriptions on the right.

_____   (a)   Internal program

_____   (b)   External program

1.   Stored in memory only when needed
2.   Always in memory when DOS is running
3.   You can write one
4.   You can buy one and add it to your system
5.   Part of DOS package from IBM

— — — — — — — — — —

(a) 2, 5; (b) 1, 3, 4, 5

8.   The internal programs are always in memory whenever DOS is running. An external program must be loaded into memory from disk each time it is used.

Which type of programs do you think would be faster to run? _____

Why? _____

— — — — — — — — — —

Internal programs; because there's no loading time

9.   (a)   Which DOS program contains the internal commands? _____

(b)   A program that's loaded from disk into memory each time it's used is

called an _____

(c)   Which type of program starts up faster? _____

— — — — — — — — — —

(a) COMMAND; (b) external program; (c) internal

10. When a disk has been prepared for use in the IBM Personal Computer, it contains a record, called the boot record, that has a very special function. Whenever the system is started up, the boot record is read into memory.

It contains a very simple program that causes the rest of DOS—IBMBIO, IBMDOS, and COMMAND—to be loaded from the disk. It then transfers control to IBMBIO. After IBMBIO does some initial work, COMMAND takes over and you're ready to go.

(a)   Boot has two major functions. What are they? _____

and _____

(b)   When you start up your system, what happens first? _____

_____

— — — — — — — — — —

(a) load the rest of DOS; transfer control to IBMBIO; (b) boot is loaded

11. In order to boot from a disk, it must contain these DOS program files: IBMBIO.COM, IBMDOS.COM, and COMMAND.COM (IBMBIO.COM is the name of the file containing the IBMBIO program; IBMDOS.COM contains the IBMDOS program; etc.). Such a disk is called a system disk, and the three files are called the system files. The disk does not need to contain any of the DOS external programs in order to be a bootable disk.

What about the boot record? Of course it must be there too. We didn't mention it because, like the disk directory and the File Allocation Table, it will be on every disk used with the Personal Computer, whether it's a system disk or not.

(a)   Which of the following are the DOS system files?

_____ A.   DOS.COM

_____ B.   IBMDOS.COM

_____ C.   IBMBIO.COM

_____ D.   BIOS.COM

_____ E.   DOSBOOT.COM

_____ F.   COMMAND.COM

_____ G.   All of the above

(b) Which of the following must be on a bootable (system) disk?

_____ A. IBMDOS.COM

_____ B. The boot record

_____ C. IBMBIO.COM

_____ D. The File Allocation Table

_____ E. A disk directory

_____ F. COMMAND.COM

_____ G. All of the above

— — — — — — — — — — —

(a) B, C, and F; (b) G

Now you know that DOS is an operating system, made up of IBMBIO, IBMDOS, and COMMAND.

Now we're going to look more closely at some items that you'll be using with DOS: the disk drives, the disks, and the files that reside on the disks.

THE DEFAULT DRIVE

12. When the system is ready to receive a command, the command processor displays a message like this:

```
A>_
```

The message (called a "prompt") tells you two things: the command processor is ready to receive a command, and the default disk drive is A. The default drive is the disk drive where DOS will look for programs and data files. For example, if A is the default drive and you enter the command COMP SOURCE1 SOURCE2, DOS will look on drive A for the COMP program as well as the two files, SOURCE1 and SOURCE2. You can change the default drive by entering the desired drive name followed by a colon. If you type this:

```
B:
```

and press Enter, the command processor responds with this:

```
B>_
```

Now B drive is the default drive and the command processor is ready for another command.

(a) Given the prompt below, which drive is the default drive? _____

    B>_

(b) Write a command to make the other drive the default drive. _____

(c) When DOS is started, which default drive is selected for you? _____

— — — — — — — — — —

(a) drive B; (b) A: (c) drive A

13. The colon is a critical part of drive selection. If you enter a drive name without the colon, the command processor doesn't know you want to select a drive. It thinks you want to run a program of that name. If it can't find any program with that name, you'll get a message like this:

```
A>B
Bad command or file name

A>_
```

The prompt you get always indicates the default drive. Because the DOS system didn't recognize B as a drive name, the A drive remained the default drive.

If you enter an invalid drive name, you'll get an error message, as in:

```
A>H
Invalid drive specification

A>_
```

For each example below, tell what happened.

(a) A>B:
   B>_

_____

(b) A>J:
   Invalid drive specification

   A>_

_____

(c)   A>B
      Bad command or file name

      A>_

—————————————————

(a) drive B was selected; (b) there is no H drive; (c) the colon was omitted and
drive A remains selected; also, no program named B exists on drive A

DISKS

14. Each side of each disk is divided into 40 tracks with 8 sectors, as you can see
here. The *tracks* are concentric rings. The *sectors* form wedges that intersect with
the tracks. You can see that sector 20, track 7, could be used to refer to a specific
drawing part of the disk. (You won't have to do this, but DOS does when it
locates files or data.) Sometimes when DOS finds something physically wrong
with a disk, it tells you the track or sector involved.

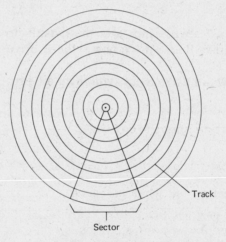

Track

Sector

Tracks and Sectors

The track nearest the outside edge is track 0, and the next is track 1. The boot
record, the disk directory, and the File Allocation Table are kept in the first part
of track 0. The rest of the disk is available to store programs and data files.

(a) What is the difference between a track and a sector? _____

_____

(b) Which track contains the boot record? _____

_____

(c) On a single-sided disk, how many tracks are available for programs and data
files? _____

– – – – – – – – – –

(a) tracks are concentric rings and sectors are wedges; (b) track 0; (c) 39 (plus part
of track 0)

15. You can protect your important disks from being written on. You do this by
covering over the write protect notch on the disk with a piece of tape.

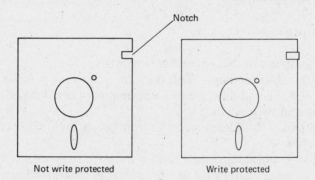

Notch

Not write protected   Write protected

Once a disk has been write protected, it cannot be written on any more (unless
you remove the tape). You can read any file on the disk, but you can't add new
files or change any files already there. Because you also can't write on the
directory, you can't erase or rename files either.

If you buy a program for your system, you may find that it is permanently write
protected by virtue of having no notch. Your DOS disk as supplied by IBM has no
notch.

Match each disk status with its allowable operations.

_____ (a) Write protected

_____ (b) Not write protected

1. Read files
2. Erase files
3. Change files
4. Rename files
5. Write new files

Label each of the following as true or false.

(c) Every 5¼-inch floppy disk has a write protect notch. _____

(d) Once a disk has been write protected, the write protection can never be removed. _____

— — — — — — — — — —

(a) 1; (b) 1, 2, 3, 4, 5; (c) false; (d) false

FILES

16. A *file* on a disk is a set of information. It may be a program, data, or such items as letters or reports. A file is anything you have called a file and stored on disk.

Every file on a disk has a unique identifier with up to three parts. Here's an example of a file identifier:

    A:CHAP1.PRN

Let's look at the parts of this identifier separately.

The first part is the drivename. This part of the filename may vary, depending on which drive holds the disk. It's not a *permanent* part of the file identifier. If used, it's followed by a colon.

The second part is the filename. It has from one to eight characters and must start with a letter.

The third part is the extension. It has from zero to three characters. Every file doesn't need an extension. But if one is used, it is separated from the filename proper with a period.

If you type a filename longer than eight characters or an extension longer than three characters, DOS truncates (chops off) the extra characters. Thus, WEDNES-DAYS.MENUS will be read as WEDNESDA.MEN.

Indicate if each name below is a valid DOS file identifier. If not, state why it is invalid.

(a) A:FILE6

    valid _____ invalid _____

(b) FILE6.SIX

    valid _____ invalid _____

(c) 6FILE.SIX

    valid _____ invalid _____

(d) FILESIXTEEN

   valid _____ invalid _____

(e) A

   valid _____ invalid _____

_ _ _ _ _ _ _ _ _ _

(a) valid; (b) valid; (c) invalid, doesn't begin with a letter; (d) this is valid but will be read as FILESIXT; (e) valid (but could be confused with drive A:)

Note: You will also see the file identifier called the file specifier or the filespec.

17. The filename and extension may be determined by the user. But DOS recognizes certain extensions and may treat them differently. Here are a few of the standard extensions.

   BAT—a file containing a set of DOS commands
   COM—one kind of external program
   EXE—another kind of external program

   DOS has other standard extensions also.
   Many files will have extensions needed by your external programs. You may have an inventory program that will work only on a file with the extension INV. You may have a mailing label program that creates a file with the extension LAB. Many of your file identifiers will have no extensions because they aren't needed for any special reasons.
   Indicate if each extension is valid or invalid. If it is invalid, tell why.

(a) COM

   valid _____ invalid _____

(b) PRACTICE

   valid _____ invalid _____

(c) DOC

   valid _____ invalid _____

(d) 6X

   valid _____ invalid _____

_ _ _ _ _ _ _ _ _ _

(a) valid; (b) valid but will be read as PRA; (c) valid; (d) valid

18. Each combination of filename and extension on a disk must be unique. That means you may have several files named TEXT1 on a disk if each has a different extension. You may also have several files with the same extension as long as each has a different filename. The drivename will be the same for each file on the same disk. You can use the same filename-extension combination on many different disks because you'll never have two disks on the same disk drive at once.

Which of the sets of complete file identifiers below represent unique names?

_____ (a)   A:TEXT1.DOC   _____ (c)   A:TEXT3.DOC
            A:TEXT1.BAK   B:TEXT3.DOC
            A:TEXT1   B:TEXT3.BAK

_____ (b)   A:TEXT2.DOC   _____ (d)   B:TEXT4.DOC
            A:TEXT2   B:TEXT3.DOC
            A:TEXT2   A:TEXT4.DOC

_ _ _ _ _ _ _ _ _ _ _

a, c, d

19. The three DOS system files are all COM files. That is, they all have the extension COM. See if you can give the complete name of the three files.

_____

_ _ _ _ _ _ _ _ _ _ _

COMMAND.COM, IBMBIO.COM, and IBMDOS.COM

Now you have learned that DOS consists of several system files and includes some external programs. You've seen the format of a disk and learned how to protect it from erasure. You've learned how to identify and change the default drive. And you can create a valid file name.

Chapter Two Self-Test

This Self-Test will help you determine if you have mastered the objectives of this chapter. Answer each question to the best of your ability, and then check your answers in the answer key at the end of the test.

1. Identify the DOS program that performs each function below:

   a. Interprets keyboard entries

   _____

   b. Performs file management

   _____

   c. Handles input and output requests

   _____

   d. Transfers control to the command processor

   _____

2. Suppose your screen shows this prompt:

   A>_

   a. What is the default drive?

   _____

   b. Write a command to switch to drive B.

   _____

   c. What does it mean if COMMAND responds

   Bad command or file name
   A>_

   _____

3. Which of the complete file identifiers below represents a file of type COM, name STEST, on drive A?

   _____ a.   A.COM.STEST

   _____ b.   A.STEST.COM

   _____ c.   A:STEST:COM

   _____ d.   A:STEST.COM

4. Which of the following must be on a disk that you boot from? (Select more than one.)

   _____ a.   IBMCOMP COM

   _____ b.   IBMBIO.COM

   _____ c.   IBMDOS.COM

_____ d. COPY.COM

_____ e. The boot record

_____ f. The DOS external programs

_____ g. COMMAND.COM

5. Match.

    _____ a. Internal programs   (1) Reside in memory after
                                            DOS is booted

    _____ b. External programs   (2) Reside on disk after
                                            DOS is booted

                                              (3) Load faster
                                              (4) Contained in COMMAND
                                              (5) You can buy or write
                                                  more of them

6. How can you protect a valuable disk from being accidentally overwritten or erased?

_____

_____

Self-Test Answer Key

Compare your answers to the Self-Test with the correct answers given below. If all your answers are correct, you are ready to go on to the Suggested Machine Exercise. If you missed any questions, you may find it helpful to review the appropriate frames before going on.

1. a. Command processor COMMAND
    b. IBMDOS
    c. IBMBIO
    d. The boot record
2. a. drive A
    b. B:
    c. You entered B without the colon
3. d
4. b, c, e, g
5. a—1, 3, 4; b—2, 5
6. Put tape over the write protect notch

Suggested Machine Exercise

In this exercise, you will practice selecting the default drive, if you have more than one drive. (If not, skip this exercise and go on to Chapter Three.)

1. Boot the system using your backup disk.
2. Try switching to drive B. (You don't need a disk in B as long as you don't enter any other DOS commands while B is the default drive.)
3. Switch back to A again.
4. Switch back and forth a few more times until you're comfortable with the process.

Now try to get some error messages.

5. Try leaving out the colon.
6. Try switching to drive X.

When you're done experimenting, shut down the system and go on to Chapter Three.

CHAPTER THREE
Typing DOS Commands

You use DOS programs by typing and entering commands. A typical command might be:

ERASE JOHNSON.LET

This command asks DOS to erase the disk file named JOHNSON.LET. There are many commands corresponding to the various DOS internal and external programs. You'll be learning the command details in later chapters. In this chapter, we will cover the general format of all DOS commands, what happens when a DOS command is entered, and some special keys you can use when typing DOS commands.

When you complete your study of this chapter, you will be able to:

- Identify the location of special keys on the Personal Computer keyboard
- Identify the control keys that invoke major DOS control functions
- Write a basic DOS command involving a program and a file
- Write DOS commands for programs that are not on the default drive
- Write DOS commands for files that are not on the default drive
- Briefly describe what happens after a DOS command is entered
- Interpret error messages resulting from DOS commands

SPECIAL KEYS

Figure 3.1 shows the layout of the Personal Computer keyboard. We will use it in the following frames.

Figure 3.1   The Keyboard

1.   Your Personal Computer keyboard contains all the keys of a traditional typewriter and many special keys as well.

The letter and number keys are laid out just like a standard typewriter. Other keys are somewhat different. If you know touch typing, you will need a little practice to adapt to this keyboard. One major difference is that any of these keys will repeat if held down.

Each letter key has an upper- and a lowercase. The uppercase—A CAPITAL LETTER—is reached by holding down a Shift key while hitting the letter key. There are two Shift keys on the keyboard, in standard typewriter positions for such keys. Each one is labeled with this symbol: ⇧.

To the right of the space bar is the CapsLock key. It is like a toggle switch; that is push it once and the shift lock is on; push it again and the shift is unlocked. You don't have to hold it down to keep it on. When CapsLock is on, all letters will type in uppercase. Numbers and other characters are not affected. The symbols over the number keys are typed by holding down a Shift key while striking the appropriate character key.

Be careful about the letter L and the number 1. The computer will not read a lowercase L as a one, even in something as "obvious" as 1985. You must use the number key in the top row for the number one. The same is true for the letter O and the number 0.

(a)   Which key is immediately to the left of the right-hand Shift key? (Choose one.)

_____ A.   ⌨ (?/ key)

_____ B.   ⌨ (? Home key)

_____ C.   ⌨ (}] key)

_____ D.   ⌨ (+ = key)

(b)   Which key is immediately to the left of the left-hand Shift key? (Choose one.)

_____ A.   F4

_____ B.   Ctrl

_____ C.   F8

_____ D.   Alt

(c)   On the Personal Computer keyboard, the letter and number keys have a much better layout than on a standard typewriter. True or false?_____

(d) Which of the following is true?

_____ A. The CapsLock key causes all letters to be uppercase, but not numbers.

_____ B. The CapsLock key causes both letters and numbers to be shifted to uppercase.

(e) Which of the following is true?

_____ A. To use CapsLock, you have to hold it down while you type the letters, just like a Shift key.

_____ B. CapsLock is turned on when you press the key once and stays on until you press it again.

(f) Which of the following is true?

_____ A. The computer will interpret the letter L as either a letter or a number, whichever is more appropriate.

_____ B. You must be careful to use the number key and not the lowercase letter L to type the number one.

_ _ _ _ _ _ _ _ _ _

(a) A; (b) C; (c) false—they have the same layout as a standard keyboard; (d) A; (e) B; (f) B

2. Computer programs tend to use more symbols than regular text, and so your keyboard has more symbols than a regular typewriter.

To the right of the left-hand Shift key is a key containing \ and I.

The comma key has < over it and the period key has > over it. These will take some time to learn if you are used to commas and periods in both the upper- and lowercase positions.

Above the right-hand Shift key is a key containing ` and ~.

Next to the P are two keys containing [{ and] }.

The standard typewriter symbols, such as ; @ and +, are also available in their usual positions.

Which of the following symbols are available on the Personal Computer keyboard?

_____ (a) ÷		_____ (d)]		_____ (g) Σ	
_____ (b) {		_____ (e) =		_____ (h) ~	
_____ (c) h		_____ (f) @		_____ (i) I	

_ _ _ _ _ _ _ _ _

b, d, e, f, h, i

3. The keyboard has several keys labeled with arrows. You have already learned to identify the Enter key, which has this symbol: ↵ , and the Shift keys, which have this symbol: ⇧ .

Above the Enter key is the backspace key, which has this symbol: ←.

Next to the Q is the tab key, which has this symbol: ⇤ . The lowercase is the forward tab represented by →| . The uppercase doesn't do anything in DOS, although it might with other programs you use.

Match the symbols with their meanings.

_____ (a) ↵   1. Backward tab
                           2. Backspace
_____ (b) →| 3. Enter
                           4. Shift
_____ (c) |←   5. Forward tab
                           6. Doesn't do anything
_____ (d) →

_____ (e) ⇧

_ _ _ _ _ _ _ _ _ _

(a) 3; (b) 5; (c) 6; (d) 2; (e) 4

4. To the right of the standard keyboard is the numeric keypad. If you are accustomed to a 10-key calculator, you may prefer to use the numeric keypad to enter numeric data. The numeric keypad consists of the digits 0 to 9, a decimal point (.), a plus sign (+), and a minus sign (−).

Notice that most of the keys have an upper- and lowercase; the numerics are the uppercase. They are *not* controlled by the Shift keys. Above the keypad is NumLock key, which controls the case of the numeric keypad. Like CapsLock, it is a toggle key. After booting, it is off. Press it once, and it is on. Press it again, and it is off. When NumLock is on, the numerics can be used. When NumLock is off, they can't. The plus and minus work in both cases.

Suppose you want to enter a lot of numeric data, and you want to use the numeric keypad. What should you do to make the numeric keypad work?

_____

_ _ _ _ _ _ _ _ _ _

turn NumLock on

5. The lowercase of the numeric keypad contains some special functions that do not work with DOS with some exceptions: the 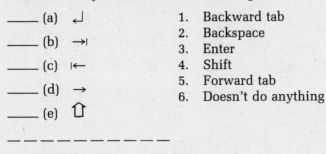 key works just like the backspace key, and, as you learned before, Del is used in the reboot process. Ins and Del also work with the DOS editor, which you'll be learning about in

Chapters Eight through Ten. The other functions work with the BASIC program supplied by IBM and may work with other programs designed for the Personal Computer. (We have a game program that uses the four arrow keys to control the position of our spaceship.)

The key in the upper right-hand corner is labeled ScrollLock on top and Break on the front face. DOS does not use the ScrollLock function, but it does use Break, which you will learn about in the next part of this chapter.

Which of the following key symbols have no function in DOS?

_____ (a) ↓	_____ (e) ←	_____ (i) I←
_____ (b) Ins	_____ (f) Del	_____ (j) ScrollLock
_____ (c) Home	_____ (g) →	_____ (k) →I
_____ (d) ↑	_____ (h) NumLock	_____ (l) End

_ _ _ _ _ _ _ _ _ _

a, c, d, g, i, j, l (b is used with the editor, e is the backspace, f is used in rebooting and with the editor, h controls the case of the numeric keypad, and k is the tab)

6. At the left of the keyboard are the ten program function keys, labeled F1 through F10. Any program can use these keys for whatever functions it likes. DOS uses F1 to F6. You will learn the functions of F1 to F6 when you study the EDLIN program (the DOS text editor) in Chapters Eight through Ten. You will also learn one function for F6 in this chapter.

Which of the following statements is true?

_____ (a) F1 to F10 have no function on the IBM keyboard.

_____ (b) Different programs make different uses of F1 to F10.

_ _ _ _ _ _ _ _ _ _

b

We have discussed all the keys on your keyboard except Esc, Ctrl, and Alt. You will learn how to use these three keys in the next section.

THE CONTROL FUNCTIONS

7. As you type a command, it is stored in a special keyboard memory area. It is not sent to the command processor until you say so. You send a command to the command processor by pressing the Enter key.

As you type a command, you may make mistakes. Before you press Enter, you can correct those mistakes. The Backspace key is used to back up the cursor so you can overtype a character. The Backspace key erases as it backspaces.

Sometimes you make so many typing mistakes in a line that it's easier to throw it out and start over than to backspace and correct it. The Escape key will eliminate the current line if you press it while typing a command. The Escape key is in the upper left and has this symbol: Esc.

When you press Esc, a backward slash is displayed on the canceled line and the cursor moves to a new line. Suppose your display looks like this:

        A>CPY B;TRX_

If you press the Esc key, your display will look like this:

        A>CPY B;TRX\
        _

You can then type a corrected line.

(a) How do you send the line you have just typed to the command processor?

_____

(b) How do you eliminate the line you just typed and start over?

_____

(c) How do you backspace and erase one character in the line you are typing?

_____

(d) Match the key names with their symbols. (Not all the symbols are used; some aren't even real keys.)

_____	A.	Backspace	1.	↳
			2.	→
_____	B.	Enter	3.	↵
			4.	⊢←
_____	C.	Escape	5.	←
			6.	↺
			7.	BS
			8.	Esc
			9.	Ent

_ _ _ _ _ _ _ _ _ _

(a) press Enter; (b) press Escape; (c) press Backspace; (d) A–5; B–3; C–8

8. Sometimes you need to type a command that is longer than the 80-character screen line. If you just keep typing, the cursor will automatically move to the beginning of the second line when it reaches the end of the first line. However, you can force the cursor to the beginning of the second line earlier than that if you wish. For this "new line" function, just use Ctrl-Enter. That is, hold down the Ctrl (control) key and press the Enter key. The cursor will move to the beginning of the next line, but your command will not be sent to the command processor.

The Control key is not a character key. It is like a Shift key; when you hold it down, it changes the effect of some of the character keys that you type.

Match these keys with their descriptions.

_____ (a)   Enter

_____ (b)   Shift-Enter

_____ (c)   Ctrl-Enter

_____ (d)   Ctrl

1.   Starts a new line but does not transmit command
2.   Transmits command to command processor
3.   No meaning; not used
4.   Changes the meanings of character keys
5.   Returns the cursor to the upper left corner

_ _ _ _ _ _ _ _ _ _ _ _

(a) 2; (b) 3; (c) 1; (d) 4

9. There are two control functions that cause data to be sent to the printer. The screen print function causes the current screen image to be printed. Screen print is the uppercase function of the key with this symbol: PrtSc. To select the screen print function, hold down the Shift key while you press the PrtSc key.

You can also use echo printing. This means that each line that is displayed on the screen is simultaneously printed. Echo printing is activated with the Ctrl-PrtSc keys. Hold down the Ctrl key and press the PrtSc key. This is a toggle function. If echo printing is off, it will be turned on. If it's on, it will turn off. (When you type a command, it is echo printed when you press Enter. When DOS displays a message, it is echo printed as it is displayed.)

What is the difference between these two functions? Screen print causes 24 or fewer lines to be printed, whatever is currently on the screen. (What you see is what you get.) Echo printing causes all future data to be displayed, until you turn it off again. You might print 5 or 500 lines.

Suppose you want to print a copy of your disk directory. Would it be better to display it first and then print the screen or to turn on echo printing and then display the directory? Echo printing is probably better for this job because the directory might be longer than 24 lines.

(a)   Match the two print functions with their descriptions.

_____ A.   Screen print   1.   Toggle function

_____ B.   Echo print   2.   Prints 24 lines or less

3.   Copies lines until you turn it off again

4.   Ctrl-PrtSc

5.   ⇧ -PrtSc

(a)   Suppose echo printing is off. How do you turn it on?

_____

(b)   OK, now it's on. How do you turn it off again?

_____

— — — — — — — — — — —

(a) A–2, 5; B–1, 3, 4; (b) use Ctrl-PrtSc; (c) use Ctrl-PrtSc

Note: If you leave echo printing on while you run other DOS programs, it will slow those programs down because it takes longer to print data than to display it. Ctrl-P also acts as an echo print toggle switch.

10.   Sometimes, after you enter a DOS command and it starts processing, you change your mind. You can terminate almost any program and return to the command processor using the break function, activated with the Ctrl-Break keys. The Break key is in the upper right corner of the keyboard. It says ScrollLock on top and Break on the front. Hold down the Control key while you press this key, and you will abruptly kill any DOS program that is running except EDLIN (the text editor) and the command processor itself. This symbol will be displayed: ^C. (The ^ symbol indicates that the Control key was used.)

Suppose you ask DOS to display a file and, as the data begins to roll onto the screen, you realize it's the wrong file. You don't have to wait until the whole file is displayed. You can cancel the command with Ctrl-Break, and then enter the correct command.

Sometimes, you just want to suspend a command without actually canceling it. For example, suppose you ask DOS to type a file that is longer than 24 lines. If you don't stop it, the beginning of the file will roll right off the top of the screen before you have a chance to read it (unless you're a very fast reader). Ctrl-NumLock can be used to suspend a program. It just stops processing, that's all. When you hit any character key, it will start again; a character key is a key that types a character, such as x or the space bar.

So to view the entire file, let about 20 lines roll onto the screen; then hit Ctrl-NumLock. Read what's there, and then restart the data again by hitting the space bar (remember, any character key will do). After another 15 or 20 lines have rolled past, suspend the program again. Continue scrolling and suspending until you have found what you're looking for or the file ends.

(a) Which keys suspend a program?

_____

(b) Which keys cancel a program?

_____

(c) How can you resume a suspended program?

_____

(d) Which function causes a return to the command processor—the suspend function or the break function?_____

(e) Suppose you enter a command to display the contents of a file, and it's going past so fast you can't read it. What keys would you hit?_____

(f) Suppose after you start reading it, you find out it's the wrong file. What keys would you hit?_____

— — — — — — — — — —

(a) Ctrl-NumLock; (b) Ctrl-Break; (c) hit any character key; (d) break; (e) Ctrl-NumLock; (f) Ctrl-Break

Note: Ctrl-C acts the same as Ctrl-Break and Ctrl-S acts the same as Ctrl-NumLock. Some people prefer Ctrl-C and Ctrl-S because they can be typed with one hand.

11. You have studied the control functions: enter, backspace, escape, new line, break, suspend, screen print, and echo print. These functions work when you are using DOS programs such as COMMAND (and the internal programs), EDLIN, and FORMAT. They may or may not work with other external programs, depending on how the programs are written.

Match each function with the keys used to activate it.

____ (a)	Enter	1.	↵
____ (b)	Backspace	2.	Ctrl
____ (c)	Escape	3.	⇧
		4.	Esc
____ (d)	New line	5.	Break
____ (e)	Break	6.	←
		7.	Numlock
____ (f)	Suspend	8.	PrtSc

(g) Which of the following is true?

_____ (A) The control functions work with all programs on the Personal Computer.

_____ (B) The control functions work with DOS programs and some other programs.

_____ (C) The control functions work with DOS programs but not with other programs.

(h) Which of the following is true?

_____ (A) Alt has no function within DOS.

_____ (B) The Alt key doesn't work.

_____ (C) Alt is used in rebooting but has no other DOS function.

_____ (D) Alt can always be used in place of Ctrl.

— — — — — — — — — —

(a) 1; (b) 6; (c) 4; (d) 2 and 1; (e) 2 and 5; (f) 2 and 7; (g) B; (h) C

GENERAL COMMAND FORMAT

Now that you know which keys to use to type your DOS commands, let's look at the format of a command.

12. To enter a DOS command you must be at command level. This means you must have a DOS prompt such as A>_ or B>_ .

The general format of a DOS command is:

d>programname operands

The *d>* indicates the command prompt that's provided by the command processor, A> or B>. You don't type this. DOS displays the command prompt and you type after it on the same line.

Programname is the name of the program you want DOS to execute. It must be either an internal command or the name of an external program on one of the drives.

If it's an external program, it must be contained in either a COM or an EXE file. COM files and EXE files are external programs that have been translated into machine language and appropriately edited by the system so that they are completely ready to be run on your computer. Their file identifiers will always be in this format: *programname.COM* or *programname.EXE.* In the DOS command you enter only the programname; don't type the ".COM" or ".EXE."

The operands indicate what data the program should use. (An "operand" is something that is operated on.) In most DOS commands, the operands specify the names of files and disk drives. For example, in TYPE NEWDATA, the filename NEWDATA is the operand. Some DOS commands do not require operands.

The command is terminated by pressing Enter, which causes the command processor to process the command.

(a) Before you can type a DOS command, what must appear on your terminal?

_____

(b) Programname must be the name of:

     _____ A. A DOS internal command

     _____ B. A COM file on one of the drives

     _____ C. An EXE file on one of the drives

     _____ D. Any of the above

     _____ E. None of the above

(c) Suppose your A disk contains these files: TRUE.COM, BLAST.EXE, and TEST.EXE. You want to run the TEST program, which doesn't use any operands. What entry do you make?

    A>_____

_ _ _ _ _ _ _ _ _ _ _

(a) DOS prompt (A> or B>); (b) D; (c) TEST

13. If an external program is not stored as a file on the default drive, you must tell DOS where to find it. You can switch to the correct drive, as in:

    A>B:
    B>CALC

You can also precede the programname with the drivename, as in:

    A>B:CALC

The major difference between these two techniques is the drive that remains active. In the first example, the B drive becomes the default drive; in the second example, the A drive remains the default drive.

For the following questions assume that your A disk contains TRUE.COM, BLAST.EXE, and TEST.EXE and your B disk contains SORT.EXE, MERGE.EXE, and LIST.EXE.

(a)   Show the entry or entries you would make if you want to run the SORT program but leave A the default drive.

A>_____

(b)   Show the entry or entries you would make if you want to run the LIST program and make B the default drive.

A>_____

— — — — — — — — — —

(a) A>B:SORT (b) A>B:
                              B>LIST

14.   Here's the general command format again:

     d>*programname operands*

Some programs, as you've seen, do not involve operands. In these cases, you just type the programname and press the Enter key.

Many programs require a file identifier as an operand. If so, after the program-name, type at least one space and then the file identifier as an operand. If the file is on the default drive, you don't need to include the drivename. For example, if you want to erase the file named SOURCE.DAT from disk A, you could enter either of these commands:

     A>ERASE SOURCE.DAT
     A>ERASE A:SOURCE.DAT

If SOURCE.DAT is on disk B, you have three choices. You could switch the disks, but this isn't very practical. You could make B the default drive, or you could enter this command:

     A>ERASE B:SOURCE.DAT

Most of the time when a command calls for a file identifier, you use both the filename and the extension. We'll let you know when the extension should be omitted.

(a)   Show the general format for a DOS command that does not require a file identifier.

d>_____

(b)   Programname is separated from operands by_____

_____

(c) In a file identifier, the drivename is:

_____ A. Always needed

_____ B. Sometimes needed

_____ C. Never needed

(d) When a file identifier is an operand, do you generally include the extension?_____

(e) Drive B is default. You want to erase the INVENTY.EXE file on disk A. Show the fastest way to do this.

B>ERASE _____

(f) Drive A is default. You want to erase DATA3.DOC, which is on the disk in drive A. Code the command.

A>_____

(g) Drive A is default. You want to type the file named PROOF.DAT, which is on drive B. Code the command.

A>TYPE _____

(h) Drive A is default. You want to use the program named COURSE, which is on drive B, and the file named STUDENTS.DAT, which is also on drive B. Code a command to do this *without* changing the default drive.

A>_____

(i) Recode the above command so that drive B becomes the default drive.

A>_____

(a) programname; (b) one or more spaces; (c) B; (d) yes; (e) B>ERASE A:INVEN-TY.EXE (f) A>ERASE DATA3.DOC or ERASE A:DATA3.DOC (g) A>TYPE B:PROOF.DAT (h) A>B:COURSE B:STUDENTS.DAT [*Note:* If you didn't code the B: with STUDENTS.DAT, DOS would look for it on the *default* drive (A), even though you coded B: with the programname;
(i) A>B:
    B>COURSE STUDENTS.DAT

15. The internal commands must not be preceded by drivenames, as they are not related to drives. (Recall that they are part of the command processor.)

(a) Which of the following will type the file named INVENTY.DAT from drive B? (TYPE is an internal command.)

_____ A. A>TYPE B:INVENTY.DAT

_____ B. A>B:TYPE INVENTY.DAT

_____ C. A>B:

   B>TYPE INVENTY.DAT

(b) Which of the following may not be prefixed with drivenames?

_____ A. Internal commands

_____ B. External commands

_____ C. File identifiers

(a) A, C; (b) A

16. For the questions below, assume that you have two disks containing these files:

Drive A	Drive B
SORT.EXE	INVENTY.EXE
MERGE.EXE	INVENTY.DAT
SORT.DAT	PARTS.DAT

(a) Show the command(s) to run the SORT program using the file named PARTS.DAT as an operand. Leave drive A as the default drive.

A>_____

_____

(b) Show the command(s) to erase SORT.DAT. (ERASE is an internal command.) Leave drive B as the default drive.

B>_____

_____

(c) Show the command(s) to run the SORT program with INVENTY.DAT as an operand. Make drive A the default drive.

B>_____

_____

—— —— —— —— —— —— —— —— —— ——

(a) A>SORT B:PARTS.DAT (b) B>ERASE A:SORT.DAT
(c) B>A:
   A>SORT B:INVENTY.DAT

17.   DOS can read upper- or lowercase. It doesn't matter whether you type a command using all capital letters, all lowercase letters, or a combination of both. Our examples will always show input commands in all capital letters so you can differentiate them from DOS messages, which are in upper- and lowercase.

   Suppose you want to enter a command to erase the file named ACTION.COM. Which one of the following would be valid?

____ (a)   A>ERASE ACTION.COM

____ (b)   A>Erase ACTION.COM

____ (c)   A>Erase Action.Com

____ (d)   A>erase action.com

—— —— —— —— —— —— —— —— —— ——

All of them are valid

DOS COMMAND PROCESSING

18.   Now that you have seen what a DOS command generally looks like, let's discuss what happens when you enter the command. First of all, DOS searches for the program you named as programname. If it's an internal program, it's already a part of the command processor. It was loaded into memory when the system was booted. Otherwise DOS looks for the appropriate EXE or COM file on the specified drive. (If no drive was specified, the default drive is assumed.)

   If it can't find the correct program, the command processor returns an error message—"Bad command or file name." DOS does not search the other drive. Below is a sample printout in which we accidentally misspelled the ERASE programname.

```
A>ERRASE INVENTY.DAT
Bad command or file name
A>_
```

This message means the system can't recognize our programname. Either we misspelled it or the appropriate COM or EXE file is not on the specified drive.

   The DOS prompt is then repeated, as shown in the above example, so that we can enter the correct command.

   Even though this error message mentions the filename, a different message is used when the operand can't be found. You'll see that message later. "Bad command or file name" always means the program can't be found.

(a) When you enter a DOS command, what's the first thing the command processor does?

_____

(b) Suppose you have the following interaction:

```
A>TYP JOHNSON.PRN
Bad command or file name
A>_
```

What could be wrong?

_____ A. TYP is not an internal command.

_____ B. JOHNSON.PRN is not a file on the A disk.

_____ C. TYP is not a program on the A disk.

— — — — — — — — — — —

(a) DOS searches for the programname program; (b) A and C

19.   If the command processor successfully locates your external program on the specified disk, it reads the program from the disk into memory. You can hear this happening. If it's a short program, it could take less than a second to load. Longer programs may take 5 seconds or longer.

DOS also stores any operands in an area of memory where the external program can find them. Control is then given to the beginning of the program. You are now out of command level and into program level.

What happens next depends entirely on the program. Most programs will check the filename(s) and other operands and display error messages if they aren't correct. You'll be learning more about this when you study the internal and external programs later on. If the operands are OK, the program may or may not display any messages. Many programs run perfectly without sending any messages to the user, as in this example:

```
A>SORT MERGDATA
      (5-second wait)
   A>_
```

During the 5-second wait, the SORT program was located, loaded, and executed. It sorted the file named MERGDATA. Then it terminated, displaying no messages.

When the program terminates, the command processor resumes control and you're back at command level again. You'll know when this occurs because you'll see the DOS command prompt. The terminated program is completely finished. There's no "residue" waiting to be reactivated. Your next command may refer to any program (even the same program all over again).

(a) Below is shown a typical DOS interaction.

```
A>MERGE B A
   (3-second wait)
A>_
```

Briefly describe what happened during the 3-second wait. (*Note:* MERGE is not an internal command.)

_____

_____

_____

_____

(b) Here's another interaction.

```
A>SORT INVENTY.DAT
   FILE NOT FOUND_
```

What program sent the error message?_____

At what level are you now?_____

Can you enter a DOS command now?_____

— — — — — — — — — —

(a) DOS searched for and loaded the MERGE program, passed the operands to it, and gave it control; the MERGE program ran and terminated and DOS resumed control; (b) SORT, program level, no (you must have the DOS prompt to enter a DOS command; you would need to press Ctrl-Break to abort the SORT program and get back to DOS command level)

Chapter Three Self-Test

You may refer to Figure 3.1 or the keyboard itself to answer questions 1 through 5.

1. Which key is next to the Ctrl key?
    a. A
    b. CapsLock
    c. Space bar
    d. ↵

2. Which key is next to the Enter key?
   a. Space bar
   b. Tab
   c.
   d. +

3. Which key is next to the NumLock key?
   a. Space bar
   b. Ctrl
   c. Shift
   d. ←

4. Which key is next to the PrtSc key?
   a. Shift
   b. Space bar
   c. Alt
   d. Esc

5. Which key is next to a Shift key?
   a. Q
   b. +
   c. NumLock
   d. \

6. Which key/s do you press for the following functions?

   a. Send a line to DOS: _____

   b. Screen print: _____

   c. Echo print: _____

   d. Suspend processing: _____

   e. Resume processing: _____

   f. Break processing: _____

   g. Back up one character: _____

   h. Start a new line without sending any characters:_____

   i. Turn on the numeric keypad: _____

   j. Turn off the numeric keypad: _____

   k. Eliminate the current line and start over: _____

7. Suppose A is the default drive and you are using two disks:

Drive A	Drive B
LIST.COM	PUSH.COM
SORT.COM	PULL.COM
MOVE.COM	INVENTRY
LETTERA	ORDERS
LETTERB	STOCK
LETTERC	

   a. Write a command to use the LIST program with the LETTERA file.

     A>_____

   b. Write a command to use the SORT program and the STOCK file.

     A>_____

   c. Write a command to use the PUSH program with the LETTERB file. Leave A the default drive.

     A>_____

   d. Write a command to use the PULL program with the INVENTRY file. Leave A the default drive.

     A>_____

   e. Write commands to use the PULL program with the STOCK file. Make B the default drive.

     _____

     _____

8. Suppose you have this interaction:

```
A>CRUSH LETTERD
Bad command or file name
A>_
```

What is wrong?_____

_____

9. Can you use a drivename with an internal command, as in

   A>B:TYPE STOCK _____

10. Suppose you have this interaction:

```
A>SORT LETTERC
    (10-second pause)
A>_
```

Briefly describe what the computer did during the 10-second pause.

_____

_____

11. Which of the following should be used to type DOS commands?
    a. Capital letters
    b. Lowercase letters
    c. Either of the above

Self-Test Answer Key

1. a
2. c
3. d
4. a
5. d
6. a. Enter (↵)
   b. Shift-PrtSc
   c. Ctrl-PrtSc
   d. Ctrl-NumLock
   e. Any character key
   f. Ctrl-Break
   g. Backspace (←)
   h. Ctrl-Enter
   i. NumLock
   j. NumLock
   k. Esc
7. a. A>LIST LETTERA
   b. A>SORT B:STOCK
   c. A>B:PUSH LETTERB
   d. A>B:PULL B:INVENTRY
   e. A>B:
      B>PULL STOCK
8. There is no CRUSH.COM or CRUSH.EXE file on the A drive.
9. No
10. The SORT program was loaded and executed.
11. c

Suggested Machine Exercise

In this exercise, you'll practice typing and entering commands. You'll enter a lot of "bad" commands, just for practice. Don't worry about that. It doesn't hurt the computer in any way.

1. Start by booting DOS.

2. Try typing the following, just to get used to the regular keyboard. Correct your mistakes with the backspace key.

   1990 is the time for 46,235.78 good people to come to the aid of their parties.

3. Enter what you have typed. You should get the message "Bad command or file name."

4. Turn on the CapsLock key and type the above again. It should come out this way:

   1990 IS THE TIME FOR 46,235.78 GOOD PEOPLE TO COME TO THE AID OF THEIR PARTIES.

5. Eliminate what you have just typed with the Esc key.

6. Turn off CapsLock.

7. Print your screen. Watch the cursor as the screen is printed. It marks off each line that is printed.

8. If the screen didn't print, check the following:

   a. Has your printer been set up properly for the Personal Computer? If not, follow the directions in your Guide to Operations, or get help from your dealer.

   b. Does your printer have power? Is the power light on? If not, is it plugged in and turned on?

   c. Is your printer on-line to the computer? Is it plugged into the computer and the printer line switch on?

   d. Is the paper loaded correctly?

   e. If you can't make screen print work, you'll need to get help from your dealer (or someone else).

9. Turn on echo printing.

10. Turn on the numeric keypad and use it to type the following:

    1230 + 456 − 789.5

11. Enter the line you just typed. It should echo print. So should COMMAND's response. (Another bad command.)

12. Practice suspending and resuming a program. The command DIR will cause your disk directory to be displayed. With echo printing on, it will display quite slowly and you'll have the chance to suspend and resume the process several times.

   a. Type and enter this command:

   A>DIR

   Remember it doesn't have to be in capital letters.

   b. Use Ctrl-NumLock to suspend it.

   c. Use any character key to resume it.

13. Use DIR again, and this time use Ctrl-Break to break it.

14. What happens if you print the screen with echo printing on? Try it. It should work just the same as before.

15. Continue practicing these functions until you feel comfortable with them. When you're ready, shut down your system and go on to Chapter Four.

CHAPTER FOUR

Internal Commands

Whenever the DOS prompt is displayed (A> or B>), the internal commands can be used. There are seven internal commands: DATE, TIME, DIR, ERASE, RE-NAME, TYPE, and COPY. (DOS version 1.0 is somewhat different.) You will study all but COPY in this chapter. COPY is taught in Chapter Five.

When you have finished this chapter, you will be able to:

- Use the DATE command to display and change the system's date
- Use the TIME command to display and change the system's time
- Use the DIR command to display all or part of a disk directory in any of three formats
- Use the ERASE command to erase one or more files from a disk
- Use the RENAME command to change the names of one or more files
- Use the TYPE command to display a file
- Interpret DOS messages associated with these built-in commands

THE DATE AND TIME COMMANDS

1. The DATE and TIME commands invoke the same functions you are familiar with from the booting procedure.

If you enter DATE with no operand, DOS will respond:

```
Current date is (whatever date DOS thinks it is)
Enter new date: _
```

You can change the date by entering a new one in DOS format or leave it alone by just pressing Enter.

TIME is very similar to DATE. If you enter TIME with no operand, DOS will respond:

```
Current time is (whatever time DOS thinks it is)
Enter new time: _
```

Like the date, you can change the time or leave it alone.

If you want to change the date or time without checking the current value, you can enter the command with the appropriate date or time as an operand. Suppose you want to change the date and time to August 1, 1985 at 7:00 a.m. You could enter:

```
A>DATE 8-1-85
A>TIME 7
A>_
```

Notice that DOS doesn't acknowledge the new date or time, other than to display a prompt for the next command. Don't worry, DOS really does change the date and time when you enter commands this way.

(a) *Review.* Which of the following are valid DOS dates?

_____ A. MAR 1, 1989 _____ D. 6/10/2016 _____ G. 12–21–1979

_____ B. 3–1–89 _____ E. 6/10/16 _____ H. 1–1–2106

_____ C. 3–1–1989 _____ F. 6–10–16 _____ I. 5–10–99

(b) *Review.* Which of the following are valid DOS times?

_____ A. 12 _____ D. 16.5 _____ G. 21.4.36

_____ B. 23:01 _____ E. 6.59.16.01 _____ H. 7:2:1.20

_____ C. 23–01 _____ F. 0 _____ I. 7/2/1.20

(c) Code a command to review the current date.

A>_____

(d) Code a command to review the current time.

A>_____

(e) Code a command to change the time to midnight.

A>_____

(f) Code a command to change the date to January 1, 2001.

A>_____

— — — — — — — — —

(a) B, C, D, I (A is in the wrong format: E and F have an illegal year; G is too early; H is too late); (b) A, B, F, H (C uses a hyphen instead of a colon; D uses a period instead of a colon; E uses periods instead of colons; G uses periods instead of colons; I uses slashes instead of colons); (c) A>DATE (d) A>TIME (e) A>TIME 0 (f) A>DATE 1–1–2001

THE DIR COMMAND

2. If you worked the machine exercise for Chapter Three, you have already used the DIR (directory) command. It causes a disk directory to be displayed.

The basic form of the command is DIR with no operands. This will cause the full directory of the default disk to be displayed, as in the printout below.

```
COMMAND  COM     4959    5-07-82   12:00p
FORMAT   COM     3816    5-07-82   12:00p
CHKDSK   COM     1720    5-07-82   12:00p
SYS      COM      605    5-07-82   12:00p
DISKCOPY COM     2008    5-07-82   12:00p
DISKCOMP COM     1640    5-07-82   12:00p
COMP     COM     1649    5-07-82   12:00p
EXE2BIN  EXE     1280    5-07-82   12:00p
MODE     COM     2509    5-07-82   12:00p
EDLIN    COM     2392    5-07-82   12:00p
DEBUG    COM     5999    5-07-82   12:00p
LINK     EXE    41856    5-07-82   12:00p
BASIC    COM    11392    5-07-82   12:00p
BASICA   COM    16768    5-07-82   12:00p
ART      BAS     1920    5-07-82   12:00p
SAMPLES  BAS     2432    5-07-82   12:00p
MORTGAGE BAS     6272    5-07-82   12:00p
COLORBAR BAS     1536    5-07-82   12:00p
CALENDAR BAS     3840    5-07-82   12:00p
MUSIC    BAS     8704    5-07-82   12:00p
DONKEY   BAS     3584    5-07-82   12:00p
CIRCLE   BAS     1664    5-07-82   12:00p
PIECHART BAS     2304    5-07-82   12:00p
SPACE    BAS     1920    5-07-82   12:00p
BALL     BAS     2048    5-07-82   12:00p
        25 File(s)
```

In this directory, the filename is in columns 1 to 8, and the extension is in columns 10 to 12. The dot that you use to precede the extension is not displayed. Thus the first file in the above directory is COMMAND.COM, and the last file BALL.BAS.

The next field in the directory tells the number of bytes in the file. The next two fields show the date and time the file was last changed. These will reflect the values of the DATE and TIME operands the last time something was written in the file. The above directory is of our DOS system disk, which we have not changed. That's why all the files have the same date and time.

Two files will never show up in a disk directory, even though they're on the disk—IBMBIO.COM and IBMDOS.COM. The boot record and the File Allocation table also don't show up.

The last line of the display tells you the number of files that were listed.

(a) Write a command to get a full directory of the disk in the default drive.

A>_____

(b) In the above sample directory, which is the largest file?

_____

(c) Which is the smallest?_____

(d) How many files are listed?_____

(e) Can you tell from the directory when the files were created?_____

(f) Which DOS files are included in a full directory of the DOS disk?

_____ A. IBMDOS.COM

_____ B. IBMBIO.COM

_____ C. COMMAND.COM

_____ D. The boot record

_____ E. All the external program files

_____ F. All of the above

_____ G. None of the above

_ _ _ _ _ _ _ _ _ _ _

(a) A>DIR (b) LINK.EXE; (c) SYS.COM; (d) 25; (e) no—just when they were last worked on; (f) C, E

3. You've seen the basic format for the DIR command; now let's look at some variations.

If you want to display the directory of the nondefault drive, you can add a drivename to the command, as in:

A>DIR B:

The above command will display the directory of the disk in the B drive.

If the directory takes longer than 24 lines, you can have it displayed one screenful at at time by adding /P (for pause) to the command, as in:

A>DIR/P

When you use /P, DOS displays 23 directory entries and a line that says, "Strike a key when ready. . . ." When you strike any character key, the next part of the directory is displayed.

If you don't need to see the size, date, and time, you can get a long directory in one screen by adding /W (for "wide") to the COMMAND, as in:

A>DIR /W

/W causes the file identifiers to be displayed five across, as shown in the printout below.

```
COMMAND    COM  FORMAT    COM  CHKDSK    COM  SYS       COM  DISKCOPY  COM
DISKCOMP   COM  COMP      COM  EXE2BIN   EXE  MODE      COM  EDLIN     COM
DEBUG      COM  LINK      EXE  BASIC     COM  BASICA    COM  ART       BAS
SAMPLES    BAS  MORTGAGE  BAS  COLORBAR  BAS  CALENDAR  BAS  MUSIC     BAS
DONKEY     BAS  CIRCLE    BAS  PIECHART  BAS  SPACE     BAS  BALL      BAS
        25 File(s)
```

/W should only be used with a monitor that has 80 characters per line.

/W and /P can be used in combination with each other and with other operands. Thus, you might enter:

A>DIR/P B:

The above command would obtain a directory of the B drive, pausing after every 23 lines. (/P and /W don't make sense together since no DOS disk has more than 125 files, and /W can display 125 file names on one screen.)

The location of /P and /W are not important. You can put them anywhere after the word DIR. Thus, all of the following are legitimate commands:

A>DIR /P B:
A>DIR B:/P
A>DIR B: /P
A>DIR /PB:

(a) Write a command to obtain a directory of the disk in drive B.

A>_____

(b) Change your above command so the directory will be abbreviated and printed five across.

A>_____

(c) Write a command to display a directory of the default drive, one screenful at a time.

A>_____

(d) Which of the following commands are legal?

_____ A. A>DIR/P B:

_____ B. A>DIR /W B:

_____ C. A>DIR B: /P

_____ D. A>DIR B:/W

_____ E. A>W/DIR B:

_ _ _ _ _ _ _ _ _ _ _

(a) A>DIR B: (b) A>DIR/W B: (you may have put the /W in some other position); (c) A>DIR/P or A>DIR /P (d) A, B, C, and D; E is illegal because DIR must come first

4. So far you have been dealing with full disk directories. Now let's look at how you can get a partial directory.

Suppose you want to find out the size of a particular file. You don't have to display the entire disk directory. You can ask for the directory entry of that file only, as in:

```
A>DIR LINK EXE
LINK      EXE 41856 5-07-82 12:00p
        1 File(s)
```

You can even get the directory of a group of files with the same filename and different extensions by specifying just the filename, as in:

```
   DIR B: LOCKMARK
LOCKMARK DAT      631     5-10-80     3:14p
LOCKMARK DOC      397     5-10-80     3:15p
LOCKMARK ASM     2485     5-10-80     3:15p
        3 File(s)
```

/P and /W can be used with filenames, although they are rarely needed.
If DIR can't find the file you request, you'll get the message "File not found."
If there's no disk in the specified drive, you'll see this message:

```
Not ready error reading drive x
Abort, Retry, Ignore?_
```

You must respond to this message with a single letter: A for abort, R for retry, or I for ignore. You should not push Enter after you type the letter. Abort cancels the command. Then you can install the proper disk and try again. Alternatively, you can install the disk while this message is displayed and then type R for Retry. Don't use the Ignore response; you might mess up your disk.

(a) Write a command to find out the date that A:SYMBOL.DAT was last worked on.

A>_____

(b) Write a command to find out the size of B:CANCEL.COM.

A>_____

(c) Write a command to find out the names (only) of all files that have the filename ROBDOG on the B drive. You suspect there may be more than 23 of them.

A>_____

(d) Suppose you have the following interaction:

```
A>DIR LINK.COM
File not found
A>_
```

What's wrong?_____

(e) Suppose you have the following interaction:

```
A>DIR
Not ready error reading drive A
Abort, Retry, Ignore?_
```

What's wrong?_____

— — — — — — — — — —

(a) A>DIR SYMBOL.DAT (b) A>DIR B:CANCEL.COM (c) A>DIR/W B:ROBDOG
(d) there is no file named LINK.COM on the A drive; (e) drive A does not have a disk installed properly

You'll learn some other techniques for displaying groups of files later in this chapter.

THE ERASE COMMAND

5. If you want to erase a file from a disk, you use the ERASE command, which has this format:

ERASE *file-identifier*

For example, to erase the file named INVENTY.DAT, you would enter A>ERASE INVENTY.DAT. To erase a file on drive B named SORTED.TMP, you would enter A>ERASE B:SORTED.TMP.

Recall that, if you don't use a file extension with the DIR command, DIR will give you all files with that filename regardless of the extension. ERASE does *not* do this. If you enter the command A>ERASE PARTICLE, only the file named PARTICLE will be erased; if the disk also contains files named PARTICLE.COM and PARTICLE.DOC, they will not be harmed. This feature is for your own protection, of course.

If ERASE can't find the file you specify, you will see the standard "File not found" message. If you forget to specify a file identifier, you will see this interaction:

```
A>ERASE
Missing file name
A>
```

Another error situation will occur if the destination disk is write protected. Here's the message:

```
Write protect error writing drive x
Abort, Retry, Ignore?_
```

A file cannot be erased from a write protected disk. Either remove the write protection tape and try again or give up trying to erase the file.

Be very careful of the ERASE command. Once you have entered the command, the file is virtually gone; you don't get a second chance.

Suppose you are working with these two disks:

Drive A	Drive B
TABLE.DAT	EXTRA
TABLE.COM	EXTRA.A
TABLE.DOC	

(a) Code a command to erase the file named TABLE.DAT.

A>_____

(b) Code a command to erase the file named EXTRA.

A>_____

(c) Suppose you have this interaction:

```
A>ERASE TABLE.D
File not found
A>
```

What went wrong?_____

(d) Suppose you have this interaction:

```
A>ERASE
Missing file name
A>
```

What went wrong?_____

_ _ _ _ _ _ _ _ _ _

(a) A>ERASE TABLE.DAT (b) A>ERASE B:EXTRA (c) there is no file named TABLE.D on the default drive; (d) you forgot to include a file identifier

THE RENAME COMMAND

6. Sometimes you need to change the name of a file. The RENAME command can be used to do this. It has this format:

RENAME *current-file-identifier new-file-identifier*

RENAME can be abbreviated REN. For example, to change the name of INVEN-TY.DAT to OLD.DAT, you would enter this command: A>REN INVENTY.DAT OLD.DAT. You can include a drivename with either file identifier, but RENAME will ignore the drivename with the new-file-identifier because you can't move a file from one disk to another with the RENAME command. Therefore, the new-file-identifier must have the same drivename as the current-file-identifier.

If you don't include an extension in the file identifier, only a filename with no extension will be renamed. You can't rename a group of files this way. As with ERASE, this is for your own protection.

RENAME requires two file identifiers. If you forget to include either of them, you'll see this message: "Missing file name." Another error message you might see is "Duplicate file name or file not found." This message means one of two things—either there is no file to match the current-file-identifier or there is already a file with the new-file-identifier. You'll have to figure out which problem you're facing and change the command accordingly. For example, suppose you are working with this disk:

Drive A

JONES585
SANDS585
PETER585
BIANC685

You want to change the last file to be named BIANC685.1. Here is the interaction:

```
A>REN BIANC685.1 BIANC685
Duplicate file name or File not found
A>
```

The problem is that the current-file-identifier and the new-file-identifier are reversed. So RENAME couldn't find a file named BIANC685.1 *and* there is already a file named BIANC685.

If the file is renamed successfully, there is no special message. Look at this interaction:

```
A>RENAME BIANC685 BIANC685.1
A>_
```

The lack of an error message means that the file was renamed as requested. You can verify this by checking the directory.

(a) Code a command to rename TEXT3 as TEXT4.

A>_____

(b) Code a command to rename B:PRACTICE as B:REAL.FIX.

A>_____

(c) What is wrong with this command? A>RENAME STALER B:SAVE

A>_____

(d) Look at this interaction:

```
A>REN CHAPTER3
Missing file name
A>
```

What went wrong?_____

(e) Look at this interaction:

```
A>REN CHAPTER3 CHAPTER5
Duplicate file name or File not found
A>
```

Which of the following could be wrong?

_____ A. There is already a CHAPTER5 on drive A.

_____ B. There is no CHAPTER3 on drive A.

_____ C. You have to spell out RENAME.

_____ d. RENAME can't find a file called CHAPTER5.

— — — — — — — — — —

(a) A>REN TEXT3 TEXT4 (b) A>REN B:PRACTICE REAL.FIX (you don't have
to specify the second drivename with RENAME, but you can if you want); (c) you
can't change the drivename with the RENAME command—RENAME will ignore
the B: in the second file identifier; (d) the *new-file-identifier* is missing from the
command; (d) A and B

THE TYPE COMMAND

7. One command you will use frequently is TYPE, which displays the contents
of a file. You use it with text files, not program files. You can tell the difference
between a text file and a program file because program files usually have one of
these extensions: COM, EXE, BIN, or BAS. It doesn't hurt to type a program file,
but the data that is displayed looks like nonsense. Also, if echo printing is on,
some form feeds (these are new page signals) may be sent to the printer, causing
paper to be wasted. Some data files also will not type properly.

Any text file can be TYPEd successfully. When you are typing a file, you may
find these control functions handy: echo print, suspend and resume, and break.

The format of the TYPE command is:

TYPE *file-identifer*

To type the file named SORTED, you would enter:

A>TYPE SORTED

To type the file named PRESENT.DOC on drive B, you would enter:

A>TYPE B:PRESENT.DOC

The most common error message with TYPE is "File not found." By now, you
know what this error message means.

(a) Code a command to display the file named CHAPTER1.TEX.

A>_____

(b) Code a command to display the file named FIRESIDE on the B drive.

A>_____

(c) Label each of the following file extensions either GOOD or BAD according
to whether or not a file with that extension would normally be typed
successfully.

A.	EXE _____		D.	(blank) _____
B.	DOC _____		E.	COB _____
C.	COM _____		F.	BAS _____

(d) Suppose you have the following interaction:

```
A>TYPE EXERCISE.D
File not found
A>
```

What went wrong?_____

(e) Suppose you want to print the file named B:FIRESIDE as it is typed. What control function would you use along with the TYPE command? _____

What keys are used to activate this function? _____

(f) Suppose you start to type a file and change your mind. What control function could you use to discontinue the output without waiting until the

end of the file? _____

What keys are used to activate this function? _____

(g) Suppose the typed file starts rolling off the top of the screen before you can read it. What control function could you use to give you a chance to read the

file?_____

What keys are used to activate this function?_____

What keys are used to let the display continue?_____

— — — — — — — — — — —

(a) A>TYPE CHAPTER 1.TEX (b) A>TYPE B:FIRESIDE (c) A—bad, B—good, C—bad, D—good, E—good, F—bad; (d) there is no file named EXERCISE.D on the A drive; (e) echo print; Ctrl-PrtSc; (f) break; Ctrl-Break; (g) suspend; Ctrl-NumLock; any character key

GLOBAL FILE IDENTIFIERS

8. A file identifier is used to identify a particular file or group of files on a disk. The file identifier is specific when it refers to a single file. A *global* file identifier may refer to a number of different files. One way of specifying a global file identifier is to use an asterisk for either the filename or extension, and the actual filename or extension for the other. *.COM refer to all the files on the disk that have extension "COM," no matter what the specific filename is.

Label the file identifiers below as specific or global.

(a) B:INVENT.DEC _____

(b) INVENT.* _____

(c) A:*.DEC _____

(d) INVENT.DEC _____

_ _ _ _ _ _ _ _ _ _

(a) specific; (b) global; (c) global; (d) specific

9. A complete file reference may include a drivename as well as a filename and extension. Either the filename or the extension, or both, can be replaced with an asterisk. The asterisk means that any combination of characters will do. The drivename cannot be replaced with an asterisk since a command can deal with only one disk drive at a time. However, the drivename can be omitted if the default drive is appropriate.

Match the file references with their descriptions.

_____ (a) *.PRN

_____ (b) JOBTIME.*

_____ (c) *:JOBTIME.PRN

_____ (d) *:*.*

_____ (e) *.*

_____ (f) B:*.COM

1. Invalid file identifier
2. Refers to all files on the default drive with extension PRN
3. Refers to all files on the default drive with filename JOBTIME
4. Refers to all files on all disk drives
5. Refers to all files on the default disk
6. Refers to all files on the default drive with extension COM
7. None of these

_ _ _ _ _ _ _ _ _ _

(a) 2; (b) 3; (c) 1; (d) 1; (e) 5; (f) 7

10. Suppose the disk in the default drive contains these files:

PAYROLL.COB	PIP.COM
PAYROLL.REL	ED.COM
PAYROLL.PRN	COPY.COM
PAYROLL.DAT	DISKTST.COM

Write file identifiers that refer to the files described below.

(a) All the files that have PAYROLL as the filename.

_____

(b) All the files that have COM as the extension.

_____

(c) The COBOL source file (extension COB) for the PAYROLL program.

_____

(d) All the files on the disk.

_____

— — — — — — — — — — —

(a) PAYROLL.* (b) *.COM (c) PAYROLL.COB (d) *.*

11.   You have seen how the asterisk is used to indicate a global file identifier. The asterisk indicates any number of ambiguous characters—up to eight for the filename or three for the filetype.

You can also use a question mark (?) as a character in a global file identifier. The question mark indicates just one ambiguous character. The reference ?TEST.DAT would be matched with any of these file identifiers: ATEST.DAT, BTEST.DAT, CTEST.DAT, etc. But it would not be matched by NEWTEST.DAT or A1TEST.DAT.

To answer the questions below, assume that your default disk contains these files:

        PAYROLLS.COM
        PAYROLL1.DAT
        PAYROLL2.DAT
        PAYTAXES.COM
        PAYTAXES.DAT
        PAYROLLS.COB
        PAYTAXES.COB

(a) Name any files that match PAYROLL?.DAT

_____

(b) Name any files that match PAY?????.COM

_____

(c) Name any files that match PAYTAXES.CO?

_____

— — — — — — — — — — —

(a) PAYROLL1.DAT and PAYROLL2.DAT; (b) PAYROLLS.COM and PAYTAXES.COM; (c) PAYTAXES.COM and PAYTAXES.COB

12. The question mark can be used to set any position in a filename or extension to refer to any character. The reference X?Z.* refers to any three-character filename that begins with X and ends with Z, no matter what the extension is. These files are all included.

XYZ
XYZ.TEM
X2Z.PRN
XAZ.B

Suppose a disk contains these files:

D330T1.WS
D330B1.WS
D330C1.WS
D331T1.WST
D331B1.WST
D330C1.TWS
PIP.COM
WS.COM

Write file identifiers to refer to the groups of files indicated below.

(a) All the files whose filenames end with T1.

_____

(b) All the files whose filenames include 330.

_____

(c) All the files with extension WS and filename ending with C1.

_____

— — — — — — — — — —

(a) D33?T1.* or ????T1.*; (b) ?330??.*; (c) ????C1.WS

13. Under DOS the filename has eight characters while the extension has three characters. A blank is considered a specific character. The file identifier COMP.COM is really COMPƀƀƀƀ.COM, where ƀ indicates a blank. The filename TESTDATA is really TESTDATA.ƀƀƀ.

If you use the global identifier P?.COM, you have really specified P?ƀƀƀƀƀƀ.COM. A matching filename will have blanks in positions 3 through 8; that is, it must be no more than two characters long. These identifiers would match: P1.COM, PT.COM, and P.COM. But the identifiers PIG.COM and PAYROLLS.COM would not match.

_____

Suppose a disk contains these files:

(1) XYZ.A	(5) XYZ	(9) X006.A
(2) XYY.A	(6) XYX	(10) X007.A
(3) XYY.B	(7) WALL	(11) X008.B
(4) XYX.B	(8) ROOM	(12) X009.C

Which files are included by each file identifier below. (You can use the numbers instead of the names.)

(a) ???.* _____

(b) ??X.* _____

(c) * _____

(d) X???????.A _____

(e) X???.B _____

(f) X??.B _____

— — — — — — — — — —

(a) 1, 2, 3, 4, 5, 6; (b) 4, 6; (c) 5, 6, 7, 8; (d) 1, 2, 9, 10; (e) 3, 4, 11; (f) 3, 4

14.   In writing global file identifiers the asterisk is really an abbreviation that fills the rest of a filename or filetype extension with question marks. Look at these examples:

> TE*.PRN   is equivalent to TE??????.PRN
> TE*.*   is equivalent to TE??????.???

Characters following an asterisk are ignored. *EE.COM is equivalent to *.COM or ????????.COM. The asterisk causes the field it appears in to be filled with question marks. This will create the global file identifier.

When naming your files, keep the global identifiers in mind. Give a group of related files names that can be accessed by global identifiers. For example, a set of files containing student scores from five different tests might be called TSCORES1, TSCORES2, . . ., TSCORES5.

(1)	TRY	(10)	PLOT.COM	(19)	CORRES.XX
(2)	PRACTICE	(11)	EDLIN.COM	(20)	CORRES.DK3
(3)	THIS.NOW	(12)	COPE.COM	(21)	BILLING.DT
(4)	ONE.CH	(13)	INVOICE.XX	(22)	SUPPLIES.DT
(5)	TWO.CH	(14)	INVOICE.WI	(23)	PROGRAM.COB
(6)	THREE.CH	(15)	INVOICE.DK	(24)	PROGRAM.REL
(7)	FOUR.CH	(16)	CORRES.WI	(25)	PROGRAM.PRN
(8)	FIVE.CH	(17)	CORRES.DK1	(26)	PROGRAM.DAT
(9)	INTRO.CH	(18)	CORR.DK2	(27)	PROGRAM.COM

Figure 4.1   Sample File Identifiers

The files in Figure 4.1 are numbered for your convenience. Indicate which files match each file identifier below.

(a) * _____

(b) T??.* _____

(c) T*.CH _____

(d) C*.* _____

(e) C*.D* _____

(f) *.WI _____

(g) *ES.D* _____

(h) P*.C* _____

(i) P* _____

— — — — — — — — — —

(a) 1, 2; (b) 1, 5; (c) 5, 6; (d) 12, 16, 17, 18, 19, 20; (e) 17, 18, 20; (f) 14, 16; (g) 15, 17, 18, 20, 21, 22, 26 (don't forget that the characters following * will be ignored); (h) 10, 23, 27; (i) 2

Now that you've learned how to write global file identifiers, let's practice some DIR, ERASE, and RENAME commands.

15.   In the DIR command the file identifier can be specific or global, as in these examples:

B:	This refers to all files on drive B.
.	This refers to all files on the default drive.
X??.*	This is a typical global file identifier.
XYZ.COM	This refers to a specific file.

Write two different commands to display the complete directory of the default drive.

(a) A>_____

(b) A>_____

What is the general effect of each DIR command below?

(c) DIR * _____

_____

(d) DIR *.* _____

_____

(e) DIR *.COM _____

_____

(f) DIR T*.PRN _____

_____

(g) DIR T?6?.PRN _____

_____

— — — — — — — — — — — —

(a) DIR (b) DIR *.* (c) list all files on the default drive with no extension; (d) list entire directory (all files) on the default drive; (e) list all COM files (extension COM) on the default drive; (f) list all PRN files with filename beginning with T on the default drive; (g) list all PRN files on the default drive that have filenames of three or four characters with T in the first position and 6 in the third

16.   Refer back to Figure 4.1. Assume drive A is default. Which of the DIR commands below will return the "File not found" message?

_____ (a) DIR CORRE.*

_____ (b) DIR PRACTICE.*

_____ (c) DIR PROGRAM

_____ (d) DIR *.CH?

_____ (e) DIR IN??.*

_____ (f) DIR IN*.*

_____ (g) DIR XYZ.COM

— — — — — — — — — —

(a) (No filename is CORRE.); (c) (no PROGRAM file identifier has a blank extension); (e) (no filename starting with IN has only four characters); (g) (no file with that name is on the disk)

17.   Use Figure 4.1 and give the numbers of file identifiers that would be included in directory listings produced by these DIR commands.

(a)   DIR PRACTICE.* _____

(b)   DIR *.CH? _____

(c)   DIR IN*.* _____

(d)   DIR CO???.* _____

(e)   DIR P*.* _____

(f)   DIR ??V*.* _____

— — — — — — — — — —

(a) 2; (b) 4, 5, 6, 7, 8, 9; (c) 9, 13, 14, 15; (d) 12, 18; (e) 2, 10, 23, 24, 25, 26, 27; (f) 8, 13, 14, 15

18.   The ERASE command can also reference a global file identifier. Refer again to Figure 4.1. How many files are removed from the disk by each ERASE command below?

(a)   ERASE PRACTICE _____

(b)   ERASE PROGRAM.* _____

(c)   ERASE CORRES.DK2 _____

(d)   ERASE *.COM _____

(e)   ERASE F*.CH _____

(f)   ERASE T??.CH _____

(g)   ERASE XYZ.COM _____

(h)   ERASE BILLING.DT _____

(i)   ERASE * _____

— — — — — — — — — —

(a) 1; (b) 5; (c) none; (d) 4; (e) 2; (f) 1; (g) none; (h) 1; (i) 2

19. All files can be erased from a disk with the command ERASE *.*. When you enter this command, DOS gives you the message "Are you sure (Y/N)?" If you type "Y," all files on the disk are erased. If you type "N," the ERASE *.* command is canceled and nothing is erased.

Suppose you have disks on drives A and B that contain these files:

Drive A	Drive B
PROGRAM.COB	TRY
PROGRAM.REL	PRACTICE
PROGRAM.PRN	THIS.NOW
PROGRAM.DAT	INVOICE.XX
PROGRAM.COM	INVOICE.DK
LOOK.COM	INVOICE.WI
EDLIN.COM	

Write commands to accomplish the following functions, working from the default drive indicated.

(a) Remove LOOK.COM from disk A.

A>_____

(b) Display the complete directory of the disk on drive B.

A>_____

(c) Remove files TRY and PRACTICE from drive B.

A>_____

(d) Change the default drive to B.

A>_____

(e) Remove all the PROGRAM files from drive A.

B>_____

(f) Remove the INVOICE files from drive B.

B>_____

(g) Display the directory for drive A.

B>_____

———————————

(a) A>ERASE LOOK.COM
(b) A>DIR B:
(c) A>ERASE B:*
(d) A>B:
(e) B>ERASE A:PROGRAM.*
(f) B>ERASE INVOICE.*
(g) B>DIR A:

20. Refer to Figure 4.1. Write commands to erase files as indicated below.

(a) Remove files (4) through (9).

A>_____

(b) Remove all files.

A>_____

(c) Remove files (16) through (20).

A>_____

———————————

(a) A>ERASE *.CH
(b) A>ERASE *.*
(c) A>ERASE COR*.* (or COR???.* or CORR*.*)

21. If you exercise some caution, you can do global renames. For example, suppose you want to rename all your TXT files as DOC files. You might enter this command: A>REN *.TXT *.DOC.

The following list shows the type of changes that will be made:

Before	After
AFILE.TXT	AFILE.DOC
BFILE.TXT	BFILE.DOC
CFILE.TXT	CFILE.DOC

Because we used asterisks for both global filenames, all the filenames were retained and only the extensions were changed.

You can also change a set of filenames but leave the extensions intact, as in: A>REN PRACTICE.* TEST.*. Here's what the results might be:

Before	After
PRACTICE.COM	TEST.COM
PRACTICE.DAT	TEST.DAT
PRACTICE.DOC	TEST.DOC

Suppose, instead of the above command, you entered A>REN PRACTICE.* TEST*.*. The extra asterisk after TEST makes a big difference:

Before	After
PRACTICE.COM	TESTTICE.COM
PRACTICE.DAT	TESTTICE.DAT
PRACTICE.DOC	TESTTICE.DOC

RENAME made up the new filenames by overlaying the new over the old, without erasing the old.

Suppose you want to change all files starting with COM to start with XXX. You would enter: A>REN COM*.* XXX*.*. Here are some sample results:

Before	After
COMMAND.COM	XXXMAND.COM
COMP.COM	XXXP.COM
COMSTAR.DOC	XXXSTAR.DOC
COMSTAR.TRA	XXXSTAR.TRA
COMSPACE	XXXSPACE

We said at the beginning of the frame that you must exercise some caution in doing global renames. The above example shows that two DOS files—COMMAND.COM and COMP.COM—have been renamed along with the files that were intended. This type of mistake can be troublesome (although it certainly can be repaired).

(a) Code a global RENAME command that will restore the above two DOS files to their rightful names without renaming the other files in the list.

   A>_____

(b) Code a command to rename all your files with extension P to extension T.

   A>_____

(c) Code a command to rename all files with filename JUNEDATA to filename JULYDATA.

   A>_____

———————————

(a) A>REN XXX*.COM COM*.COM
(b) A>REN *.P *.T
(c) A>REN JUNEDATA.* JULYDATA.*

Chapter Four Self-Test

This Self-Test will help you determine if you have mastered the objectives of this chapter. Answer each question to the best of your ability. Then check your answers in the answer key at the end of the test.

(1)	MOVE.COM	(8)	SUPPLY.FIL	(15)	SALES.DOC
(2)	EDLIN.COM	(9)	COPY.DOC	(16)	SALES.HST
(3)	SPEND.COM	(10)	SUPPLY.DOC	(17)	SALES.FIL
(4)	SUPPLY.ASM	(11)	RECORDS.LOC	(18)	ST.LST
(5)	SUPPLY.REL	(12)	RECORDS.STT	(19)	ST.DOC
(6)	SUPPLY.PRN	(13)	RECORD.ORD	(20)	DISK.DOC
(7)	SUPPLY.COM	(14)	RECL.AV		

Figure 4.2   Files on Drive B

   These questions are based on the disk containing the files shown in Figure 4.2. Note that this disk is in drive B.

1.   Write a command to display the entire directory.

   A>_____

2.   Write a command to display all directory entries with filenames beginning with S, no matter what the extensions are.

   A>_____

3.   Write a command to remove all DOC type files from drive B.

   A>_____

4.   Write a command to change the name of RECL.AV to REC.ASM.

   A>_____

5.   Write a command to display the contents of file SUPPLY.FIL on the console.

   A>_____

6.   Suppose SUPPLY.FIL contains about 200 lines of data. How can you stop the display after the first few lines?

   _____

7. Write a command to change all files with filename SUPPLY to filename ONHAND.

   A>_____

. 8. Write a command to display the computer's current time.

   A>_____

9. Write a command to change the current date to 01-01-2001.

   A>_____

10. Suppose the A drive contains 60 files. Code a command to display the full file directory, stopping after each screenful.

   A>_____

11. Recode the above command so that the entire directory of file identifiers will be displayed on one screen.

   A>_____

Self-Test Answer Key

1. A>DIR B:
2. A>DIR B:S*.*
3. A>ERASE B:*.DOC
4. A>REN B:RECL.AV REC.ASM
5. A>TYPE B:SUPPLY.FIL
6. Use the suspend function (Ctrl-NumLock) or the break function (Ctrl-Break)
7. A>REN B:SUPPLY.* ONHAND.*
8. A>TIME
9. A>DATE 1/1/2001
10. A>DIR/P
11. A>DIR/W

Suggested Machine Exercise

In this machine exercise, you'll get a chance to use the DATE, TIME, RENAME, and DIR commands. You won't use ERASE and TYPE until the end of the next chapter.

1. Boot DOS using your backup disk.
2. Get a directory of the boot disk.
3. Get a second directory using the /P option.
4. Get another directory using the /W option.
5. Get a directory of just the COM files.
6. Get a directory of just the BAS files.
7. Try each of the above directories (items 5 and 6) using the /W option.
8. Check the date.
9. Check the time.
10. Change the date to 12-31-99 (the last day of 1999).
11. Change the time to 23:59:59 (one second before midnight).
12. Now check the time.
13. Check the date again. It should have changed to January 1, 2000.
14. Try renaming all the BAS files to be XXX files.
15. Get a directory to see the changed file identifiers.
16. Now change those extensions back to BAS again.
17. Get a directory to make sure you successfully changed all XXX files back to BAS files.
18. Rename PIECHART.BAS to EXERCISE.
19. Get a directory of all files starting with EXER. EXERCISE should show up in this directory.
20. Change EXERCISE back to PIECHART.BAS again.
21. Continue experimenting with DIR, RENAME, DATE, and TIME until you are completely comfortable with these commands. Then shut down your system and go on to Chapter Five.

CHAPTER FIVE

The COPY Command

COPY is an internal command that is used to copy a file from one place to another. You might make a copy from one disk to another, or from the keyboard to the disk, from a disk to the printer, and so forth. You can also use copy to combine two or more files into one file; we call this concatenation.

When you have finished this chapter, you will be able to:

- Use the COPY command to make copies of one or more files
- Use the COPY command to copy several files into one file
- Use the COPY command to create a new file on a disk
- Use the COPY command to print one or more files
- Use the COPY command to change the date and time associated with a file
- Interpret DOS messages associated with the COPY commands

USES OF COPY

1.   One of the most frequent functions you will use with DOS is to copy files from one place to another. The COPY command is used to do this. Let's look at some of the types of copies you might want to make.

You might want to copy a file from one disk to another. You can copy from drive A to B or from drive B to A. Why would you do this? Here are some examples:

- Suppose you have just spent a lot of time creating a file. You're going to use the file now, but first you want to make a backup copy (called a *vault* copy), just for safety's sake. A lot of things go wrong with disks—they get coffee spilled on them, they get scratched, and so forth. It's wise to keep vault copies of all your important files. (Most computer users ignore this advice until they ruin their first disk. Then they develop some type of system for keeping vault copies of *all* their files.)
- Suppose you have a program file on a disk that is so full of other data that the program no longer can store its data on the disk. You might want to copy the program file to a disk that is otherwise empty.

- Suppose you want to ship some files to another person who has a Personal Computer. You can use COPY to make up the disk to be shipped.

As you will soon discover, there are many more reasons to copy files from one disk drive to another. These are just a few examples.

You might also find occasion to make a second copy of a file on the same disk. Here are some examples:

- Suppose you have a file containing a letter to your congressperson. You want to send the same letter to your senator, with some minor changes. Rather than typing out the second letter from scratch, you can copy the first letter and then simply change the copy. Any time you are creating a file that is similar to an existing file, you can copy the existing file and make changes to the copy.
- Suppose you are going to make changes to a file that you use all the time. Make a backup copy of the file on the same disk before you begin editing it, just for safety's sake. If you goof up the file while you are changing it, you can fall back to the backup copy. Once the file has been successfully edited, you can erase the backup file.

You may also want to copy a file from a disk to another device. For example, one way to print a file is to copy it from the disk to the printer. One way to display it on the system monitor is to copy it from the disk to the monitor. If you are using some type of auxiliary device, you might use COPY to send a file to that device.

You can also go in the opposite direction. That is, you can copy a file from another device to a disk. For example, one of the ways to create a new file is to copy it from the keyboard to a disk. (You will do so at the end of this chapter.) If you have an auxiliary device capable of input, you might want to copy a file from the auxiliary device to a disk.

Finally, you might want to copy a file from one nondisk device to another. For example, you might want to go from the keyboard to the printer or an output auxiliary unit. All these processes are possible with the COPY command.

(a) Which of the following are possible with the COPY command?

_____ A. Keyboard to disk   _____ G. Auxiliary to print

_____ B. Disk A to disk B   _____ H. Print to disk

_____ C. Disk B to disk B   _____ I. Keyboard to print

_____ D. Disk to keyboard   _____ J. Disk to print

_____ E. Auxiliary to keyboard   _____ K. Disk B to disk A

_____ F. Keyboard to auxiliary   _____ L. Disk to auxiliary

(b) Suppose you spend four hours at the keyboard creating a new file. What should you do before you remove the disk from the drive?

_____

(c) How can you create a new disk file using the COPY command?

_____

(d) Suppose you're going to make some changes to a very important file. What should you do first, for safety's sake?

_____

— — — — — — — — — —

(a) A, B, C, F, G, I, J, K, L (D and E are wrong because the keyboard is not capable of receiving output data; H is wrong because the printer is not capable of sending data); (b) make a vault copy; (c) copy from keyboard to disk; (d) make a backup copy

COPY FORMAT

2. The format of the COPY command is:

COPY *source destination*

Source indicates the input location—the place the file is to be taken from. It might be a file or an input device. *Destination* indicates the location of the new copy; it might be a file or an output device. Either *source* or *destination* may be an identifier of a disk file or one of the following:

CON   This stands for "console." On the source side, it's the keyboard, and on the destination side it's the monitor.

AUX   This stands for any device attached to whatever port is designated as AUX ("auxiliary"). This device may also be called COM.

Destination might also be one of the following:

LPT1 ⎫
LPT2 ⎬   These stand for line printers 1, 2, or 3. If you have only one
LPT3 ⎭   printer, use LPT1. You may also use PRN.

A: This can be used only when the source is a file on drive B. A file of the same name will be created on drive A.

B: This can be used only when the source is a file on drive A. A file of the same name will be created on drive B.

The special device names—CON, AUX, and LPT1 through LPT3—may be followed by colons as the drivenames are. Thus, CON: is the same as CON, AUX: is the same as AUX, and LPT1: is the same as LPT1. None of these special names can be used as file identifiers.

Let's walk through some sample COPY commands.

A>COPY FANGLES B:

This command copies a file named FANGLES from drive A to drive B. Its name will be FANGLES on the B drive also.

A>COPY FANGLES FLUGLES

This command makes a copy of the file named FANGLES. The copy, also on drive A, is called FLUGLES.

A>COPY CON KEYFILE

This command copies a file from the keyboard to the disk in drive A, where it is called KEYFILE. Note that whenever a file identifier is used, it is assumed to be a disk file.

A>COPY B:KEYFILE LPT1:

This command prints the file named KEYFILE from drive B. The colon after LPT1 is optional.

If you leave out the *destination* operand, the default drive is assumed.

A>COPY B:LOCKFILE

This command copies the file named LOCKFILE from drive B to drive A (the default). It will also be called LOCKFILE on drive A.

B>COPY A:SOMEDATA

This command copies the file named SOMEDATA from drive A to drive B (the default). It will also be called SOMEDATA on drive B.

A>COPY SOMEDATA

This command would result in an error message because you can't have two files with the same name on the same disk. The command implies that A:SOMEDA-TA should be copied as A:SOMEDATA.

(a) Code a command to copy the file named EXERA from drive A to drive B.

A>_____

(b)   Code a command to make a backup copy of EXERB from drive B. Call the copy EXERB.BAK and place it on the B drive.

A>_____

(c)   Code a command to print a copy of EXERB from drive B.

A>_____

(d)   Code a command to copy a file from the auxiliary device to the monitor.

A>_____

(e)   Which of the following cannot be used as file identifiers?

_____ A.   COPY   _____ D.   LPT1

_____ B.   CON   _____ E.   AUX

_____ C.   KBD   _____ F.   MON

(f)   Code a command to copy EXERF from drive B to the default drive. Give it the same name on the default drive.

A>_____

(g)   What is wrong with this command: A>COPY TWOSONGS?_____

_____

— — — — — — — — — — — —

(a) A>COPY EXERA B: (b) A>COPY B:EXERB B:EXERB.BAK
(c) A>COPY B:EXERB LPT1 (d) A>COPY AUX CON (e) B, D, E;
(f) A>COPY B:EXERF (g) you can't copy from A: to A: without changing the filename

3.   You can add /V to the COPY command to cause the data to be verified as it is copied. When you use /V, DOS compares each destination sector, as soon as it is written, to its source sector. If a mistake is found, it is corrected immediately. This gives the /V option an advantage over the COMP program, which merely identifies, but does not correct, errors.

If you use the /V option, you can put it anywhere after the word COPY in the command. All of the following are valid:

```
A>COPY/V TOUCAN B:
A>COPY /V TOUCAN B:
A>COPY TOUCAN/V B:
A>COPY TOUCAN /V B:
A>COPY TOUCAN B:/V
A>COPY TOUCAN B: /V
```

Code a command to copy the file named EXERA from drive A to drive B, and verify the copy.

A>_____

— — — — — — — — — — —

A>COPY/V EXERA B: (you could have put the /V anywhere after the word COPY)

KEYBOARD TO DISK

4. One way to create a new disk file is with the COPY command. Suppose we want to create a file named ADDRESES on drive A. We would enter:

    A>COPY CON ADDRESES

COPY responds by moving the cursor to the next line and waiting for us to enter data for the file. We can type and enter as many lines as we want. Here's what our example looks like after we have entered ten lines:

```
A>COPY CON ADDRESES
ADAMS 216 CAROB COURT
ANSON 3451 LOUISA DR
BECHT 15E CELERON ST
COUSINS 2121 RIDGEFIELD AV
DREW 195 BROADWAY RD
EGGARS 616 STONEHENGE WAY
ENGELS 7795 PRESTON BLVD
EPHRON 489 COMMERCE AV
FINGAL 56 HAGSTROM RD
FOCHMEIER 100 A STREET
_
```

The ten lines have been saved in memory but have not yet been written on the disk. To end the file and cause it to be written on the disk, we must enter an end-of-file symbol, which is Ctrl-Z. It displays on the screen as ^Z. There are two ways to type it. The two keys, Ctrl and Z, can be used or you can press the F6 key on the left side of the keyboard. F6 generates an end-of-file signal, which displays as ^Z.

Once Ctrl-Z has been typed and entered, COPY writes the file on the disk, and the copy function is over.

(a) Code a command to create a new file on the B drive named TALENTS.

    A>_____

(b) Code a command to create a new file on the A drive named DINARO.

A>_____

(c) How do you end a file that you create this way?

_____

(d) Which program function key will generate an end-of-file signal?

_____

(e) Describe at least two ways to get a printed copy of the file you create.

_____

_____

_____

— — — — — — — — — —

(a) A>COPY CON B:TALENTS (b) A>COPY CON DINARO (c) enter Ctrl-Z (^Z);
(d) F6; (e) use echo print while you make the file; TYPE the file with echo print
after it's made; COPY the file to LPT1 after it's made

COPY MESSAGES

5.   Now let's talk about some of the messages from COPY.

If the copy gets made successfully, you'll see this message: 1 File(s) copied.
(Later on in this chapter, you'll learn how to copy more than one file with one
command.)

If the destination drive already contains a file with the specified name, that file
will automatically be overlaid, with no warning! You'll see this message: 1
File(s) copied. It's wise to check your destination disk before submitting (entering) the COPY command.

A file can't overlay itself. If you accidentally enter a command that implies
such a copy, as in A>COPY FAULTS, you'll see this message:

```
       File cannot be copied onto itself
              0 File(s) copied
```

If the source file can't be found, you'll see this message: 0 File(s) copied.

If there isn't enough room for the file on the destination disk, you'll see this
message:

```
       Insufficient disk space
              0 File(s) copied
```

If you specified AUX as the source and no auxiliary device exists, the message "Aux I/O error" repeats and repeats until you interrupt it with the break function. If you specify AUX as the destination device and no auxiliary device exists, COPY says it makes the copy, but of course no copy is made.

If you specify LPT1 as the source device, which is impossible, you'll see this message: 0 File(s) copied. If you specify LPT1 as the destination and the printer is not hooked up and ready to go, the message "Out of paper" will be repeated until you use the break function.

Here are two messages you have seen before:

```
Not ready error reading (or writing) drive x
Abort, Retry, Ignore?
```

and

```
Write protect error writing drive x
Abort, Retry, Ignore?
```

The first message indicates that there is no disk in the specified drive. The second message indicates that the destination disk is write protected. A, for abort, is the only proper answer here. DO NOT replace the disk in the destination drive and hit R, for Retry. A quirk in the software will copy the source *directory* onto the destination *directory*, effectively destroying the data on the destination disk.

(a)   Suppose you have this interchange:

```
A>COPY COMMAND.COM
File cannot be copied onto itself
        0 File(s) copied
A>_
```

What's wrong?_____

(b)   Suppose you have this interchange:

```
A>COPY EXB B:
        0 File(s) copied
A>_
```

What's wrong?_____

(c)   Suppose you have this interchange:

```
A>COPY EXB LPT1
Out of paper
Out of paper
Out of paper
....etc.....
```

What's wrong?_____

How can you make COPY stop saying "Out of paper"?

_____

(d) Suppose you have this interchange:

```
A>COPY EXB B:
Insufficient disk space
        0 File(s) copied
```

What's wrong?_____

(e) Suppose you have this interchange:

```
A>COPY LOCKMARK.DAT B:

Not ready error reading drive B
Abort, Retry, Ignore?
```

Which of the following moves are safe?

_____ A. Type A, then fix the disk in drive B.

_____ B. Fix the disk in drive B, then type R.

_____ C. Fix the disk in drive B, then type I.

(f) Suppose you have this interchange:

```
A>COPY LOCKMARK.DOC B:

Write protect error writing drive B
Abort, Retry, Ignore?
```

Which of the following moves are safe?

_____ A. Type A, then fix the disk in drive B.

_____ B. Fix the disk in drive B, then type R.

_____ C. Fix the disk in drive B, then type I.

_ _ _ _ _ _ _ _ _ _

(a) you need to specify a destination other than A:COMMAND.COM; (b) A:EXB couldn't be found; (c) the printer isn't ready to receive data; hit Ctrl-Break; (d) the file won't fit on disk A; (e) A and B; (f) A only

SINGLE-DRIVE COPIES

6. We've described disk-to-disk copies involving two drives. If you have only one drive, you can still copy files from one disk to another. Just let A: stand for the first disk, and B: the second disk. Below is an example of the interchange between us and the computer for a single-drive, disk-to-disk copy:

```
A>COPY PRZAP B:
```
> *(Note: COPY locates A:PRZAP and copies it into memory.)*
```
Insert diskette for drive B:
and strike any key when ready
```
> *(Note: We remove the A disk, insert the B disk, and hit a key; COPY copies the file from memory onto the B disk.)*
```
        1 File(s) copied

    A>_
```

At this point, although the prompt is shown, DOS knows that the B disk is still installed in drive A. The next command involving the A disk will cause this message: "Insert diskette for drive A: and strike any key." Here's an example:

```
A>DIR
Insert diskette for drive A:
and strike any key_
```

When we hit a key (whether we changed the disk or not), DOS makes note of the fact that the A disk is now installed and continues with the directory.

Code a command to copy BELLOWS from the installed disk to another disk on a single-drive system.

```
    A>_____
```

```
A>COPY BELLOWS B:
```

CONCATENATION

7. You can use the COPY command to *concatenate* files. This means that you copy two or more files together to create one file. Use a plus sign (+) to indicate the source files you want to combine or concatenate. You may put spaces around the + or not, as you wish. Here's an example:

```
A>COPY LEFT + RIGHT WHOLE
        1 File(s) copied
```

The new WHOLE file contains first LEFT and then RIGHT. You can concatenate as many files as you want this way, as long as the destination disk has room for the new file. To concatenate five files, CHAP1 through CHAP5, you would code:

A>COPY CHAP1+CHAP2+CHAP3+CHAP4+CHAP5 REPORT

The handling of end-of-file markers gets a little tricky when concatenation is involved. Basically, there are two types of files: text files and program files. Text files are also known as ASCII files because they are recorded in the American Standard Code for Information Interchange. (ASCII is pronounced "ASK-ey.") An ASCII file ends with a Ctrl-Z character, as you learned earlier in this chapter. Program files (extensions COM, EXE, BAS, etc.) are not recorded in ASCII; their recording method is called binary, and program files are often called binary ("BY-nary") files. There is no end-of-file marker in binary files. In fact, a binary file may contain many Ctrl-Z characters, but they do not signal the end of the file. DOS finds the end of a program file by examining the file size in the disk directory.

If you do an ordinary copy, without concatenation, the whole file is copied regardless of type. Thus, an ASCII file ends up with an end-of-file mark and a binary file doesn't. If you concatenate files, DOS assumes that ASCII files are involved and handles them this way: Each source file is copied up to, but not including, the end-of-file mark. An end-of-file mark is placed at the end of the destination file. Thus, the destination file winds up with just one end-of-file mark, and it's in the right place—for an ASCII file. But this treatment is all wrong for binary files. It chops each binary source file off at the first Ctrl-Z and adds a meaningless character to the end of the destination file. The resulting file is pure garbage.

To avoid this problem, you can use /B (for binary) when you concatenate program files. /B tells COPY to ignore end-of-file markers and use the file sizes from the directory. Here's an example:

```
A>COPY/B LINK.EXE + MORTGAGE.BAS
        1 File(s) copied
A>
```

If, for some strange reason, you want to mix ASCII and binary files together, you can use /A for files that should be given ASCII treatment. /A and /B will pertain to the filenames they're coded with and all files to the right until another /A or /B is encountered. Here's an example:

A>COPY A.COM/B+B.COM+C.COM+A.DOC/A+B.DOC MIXUP

A.COM, B.COM, and C.COM will be treated as binary files because of the /B after A.COM. A.DOC, B.DOC, and MIXUP will be treated as ASCII files because of the /A after A.DOC. This is not a good idea; MIXUP, which looks to DOS like an ASCII file because it doesn't have an extension of COM, EXE, or BAS, might have several Ctrl-Zs in it. The COPY and TYPE commands would not work properly with this file.

(a) Code a command to concatenate TRUE and FALSE into a new file named LOGIC.

A>_____

(b) Code a command to concatenate PARTS from the A drive and PARTS from the B drive into a new file called TOTPARTS. Put TOTPARTS on the A drive.

A>_____

(c) Change your command above to put TOTPARTS on the B drive.

A>_____

(d) Code a command to concatenate FIRST.COM, SECOND.COM, and THIRD.COM into a file named STAY.COM. Watch out—these are program files.

A>_____

— — — — — — — — — —

(a) A>COPY TRUE+FALSE LOGIC (b) A>COPY PARTS+B:PARTS TOT-PARTS (c) A>COPY PARTS+B:PARTS B:TOTPARTS (d) A>COPY/B FIRST.COM+SECOND.COM+THIRD.COM STAY.COM

8. You can concatenate files into one of the concatenated files. That is, you can concatenate AFILE, BFILE, and CFILE together and put the new file in AFILE. The effect is the same as if you added BFILE and CFILE to the end of AFILE. To do this, simply specify or imply that the first file is the destination file, as in:

    A>COPY AFILE+BFILE+CFILE

or

    A>COPY AFILE+BFILE+CFILE AFILE

or

    A>COPY B:FIRST+B:SECOND B:

or

    A>COPY B:FIRST+B:SECOND B:FIRST

Code a command to add LOSTFILE to FOUND.

A>_____

— — — — — — — — — —

A>COPY FOUND+LOSTFILE or A>COPY FOUND+LOSTFILE FOUND

9.   When you copy a file without concatenation, the date and time of the source file are also copied. That is, the copy does not receive the current date and time. If the date and time attached to the source file are 3–15–87 at 12:15:16.02, the date and time of the destination file will also be 3–15–87 at 12:15:16.02.

Concatenation is different. When you use COPY to create a new file by concatenating two or more source files, the new file will have the current date and time. Thus, if you merge BFILE and CFILE into AFILE, the date and time associated with AFILE will be revised.

If you want to copy a file and force the copy to have a new date and time, you can *pretend* to concatenate it, as in:

   A>COPY B:WORDWRAP+

This will copy WORDWRAP from drive B to the default drive; the current date and time will be associated with A:WORDWRAP.

If you want to do the above but specify a name (or drive) for the destination file, code two commas after the plus sign. The commas signal DOS that there are no more files to concatenate. Here is an example:

   A>COPY B:WORDWRAP+,, B:NEWWRAP

This will make a copy of WORDWRAP called NEWWRAP, which will be associated with the current date and time. If the two commas were omitted, DOS would try to concatenate NEWWRAP into WORDWRAP instead.

You can force the date and time for an existing file to be updated by doing the above with the same source and destination, as in:

   A>COPY B:WORDWRAP+,, B:

(a) In which cases does DOS assign the current date and time to a file?

   _____ A.   Whenever you make a change to a file

   _____ B.   Whenever you copy a file

   _____ C.   Whenever you concatenate a file

(b) Code a command to copy FORCEFLD from drive A to drive B. The new copy should have the current date and time.

   A>_____

(c) Code a command to copy QUASARS from drive B to drive A. The new copy should have the current date and time.

   A>_____

(d) Code a command to update the date and time associated with PLANTERS on drive A.

   A>_____

_ _ _ _ _ _ _ _ _ _

(a) A, C; (b) A>COPY FORCEFLD+,, B: (c) A>COPY B:QUASARS+ (d)
A>COPY PLANTERS+,, A: or A>COPY PLANTERS+

10. When concatenating, if any source file cannot be found, DOS just skips that
file and goes on. No warning message is displayed.
 Suppose you have this interaction.

```
A>COPY BIGFILE + AFILE + BFILE
        1 File(s) copied
A>
```

Do you know that all three files were found and copied?_____

_ _ _ _ _ _ _ _ _ _

No (DOS would not warn you if it couldn't find AFILE or BFILE)

GLOBAL FILE IDENTIFIERS

11. Some COPY commands can reference global file names. For example, here
is a typical interaction:

```
A>COPY *.COM B:
PRACTICE.COM
ENTRY.COM
EDLIN.COM
MOVE.COM
DITTO.COM
MULCH.COM
ZAP.COM
        7 file(s) copied

A>_
```

The message tells you exactly which files matched the global identifier. In the
above example, there were seven COM files on the default drive.

Here's another example:

```
A>COPY B:STAR*
START1
START2
STARKEY
STARBATL
        4 File(s) copied

A>_
```

This command says to copy all files from the B drive whose names start with STAR and have no extension to the default drive.

Here's another example:

```
A>COPY *.* LPT1
        1 File(s) copied

A>_
```

This command says to copy all the files from the default drive to the line printer. This has some advantages over TYPE because TYPE won't recognize a global file identifier. The system concatenates the destination file before printing it, which is why the message indicates only one file was copied.

(a) Code a command to copy all the files from drive B to drive A.

A>_____

(b) Code a command to copy all the files with no extension from drive A to drive B.

A>_____

(c) Can you use a global file identifier with TYPE?_____

— — — — — — — — — — —

(a) A>COPY B:*.* (b) A>COPY * B: (c) no (actually you can, but TYPE will display only the first file it finds)

12. You can use global file identifiers to concatenate files. If you specify a global source and a single destination, all the matching source files will be concatenated to create the destination file. Here is an example:

```
A>COPY *.DAT ALL.DAT
```

This will concatenate all the files on disk A with extension DAT. The result will be called ALL.DAT. The order of the concatenation will be the order that DAT files are found on the disk. If the disk already contains an ALL.DAT, the other DAT files will be concatenated into it. In such cases, you may see this message: "Content of destination lost before copy." Don't panic. What it means is this: ALL.DAT was set up as the destination file. The first DAT file was added to it. The next DAT file was added to that. And so forth. Then, DOS found ALL.DAT as a *source* file because of the global identifier *.DAT. DOS finds it impossible to use ALL.DAT as both source and destination in a concatenation, and so it issues the above (somewhat cryptic) message, skips over ALL.DAT as a source file, and goes on to the next source file. No harm has been done, since the original ALL.DAT remains as the first part of the new file.

You can also do a *parallel* concatenation using global identifiers. Here's how a parallel concatenation works: Files with like filenames and different extensions are concatenated together. In the following example, we're concatenating DAT files with CAT files to create FAT files:

LOST.DAT + LOST.CAT = LOST.FAT
FOUND.DAT + FOUND.CAT = FOUND.FAT
TRUE.DAT + TRUE.CAT = TRUE.FAT
FALSE.DAT + FALSE.CAT = FALSE.FAT

The command to accomplish the above is A>COPY *.DAT + *.CAT *.FAT. This is the only instance where it is appropriate to use a global file identifier as a *destination* in a COPY command.

(a) Code a command to concatenate all the files with filename PARTS and send the new file to the line printer. (Don't store the concatenated version on disk.)

A>_____

(b) Code a command to concatenate all the files that start with P3. Name the new file PROJECT3.

A>_____

(c) Code a command to do a parallel concatenation. Matching files with extensions B1, B2, and B3 should be concatenated together and placed in files with extension ALL.

A>_____

(d) What does the message "Content of destination lost before copy" mean?

_____ A. The destination file has been accidentally destroyed and the copy is no good.

_____ B. The destination file has been changed through concatenation.

_____ C. There is something wrong with the destination file and you should erase it immediately.

- (e)   When do you use a global destination identifier?

_____ A.   Never

_____ B.   Anytime you want

_____ C.   Only when doing parallel concatenations

— — — — — — — — — —

(a) A>COPY PARTS.* LPT1 (b) A>COPY P3*.* PROJECTS (c) A>COPY
.B1+.B2+*.B3 *.All (d) B; (e) C

Now you have learned how to use the COPY command to copy individual files
from one device to another. You have also learned how to concatenate files with
the COPY command.

Chapter Five Self-Test

1.   Write a command to produce a printed copy of SUPPLY.FIL on the line
printer.

A>_____

2.   Can you write a command to display all files with type FIL on the monitor?

_____ If so, show the command.

A>_____

3.   Write a command to make a backup copy of the B disk on A. Verify the
copy.

A>_____

4.   Change your above command so the backup copy has the current date and
time.

A>_____

5.   Write a command to create a new file on the B drive named SELFTEST. You
will enter the file from the keyboard.

A>_____

6.   How will you indicate to DOS that you want to end the above file?

A>_____

7.   Write a command to concatenate all the SALES files together. Call the
result SALES.TOT.

A>_____

8. Write a command to append RECORDS.ORD to RECORDS.LOC. Verify the copied data.

   A>_____

9. Write a command to concatenate all the COM files on drive B into one file called PROGRAMS.COM.

   A>_____

10. Suppose the A drive contains these files:

LOST.A	FREE.A	HOLDINGS.A
LOST.B	FREE.B	HOLDINGS.B
FOUND.A	SPENT.A	
FOUND.B	SPENT.B	

    You want to concatenate files with matching filenames calling the results: filename.ALL. Write the command to do this.

    A>_____

11. In which of the following cases should you *not* hit "R" for "Retry"?
    _____ a. Not ready error reading drive B

        Abort, Retry, Ignore?

    _____ b. Write protect error writing drive B

        Abort, Retry, Ignore?

12. Can you do a disk-to-disk copy with only one disk drive?_____

Self-Test Answer Key

1. A>COPY B:SUPPLY.FIL LPT1 (You could also use TYPE with Ctrl-PrtSc)
2. yes; A>COPY *.FIL CON
3. A>COPY/v B:*.* A:
4. A>COPY/v B:*.*,, A:
5. A>COPY CON B:SELFTEST
6. enter Ctrl-Z (F6)
7. A>COPY SALES.* SALES.TOT
8. A>COPY/v RECORDS.LOC+RECORDS.ORD
9. A>COPY B:*.COM/B PROGRAMS.COM
10. A>COPY *.A+*.B *.ALL
11. b
12. yes

Suggested Machine Exercise

1. For this exercise, you will need a blank disk that has been properly formatted to be used with your Personal Computer. To format a disk, do this:

    a. Start up the system with your backup disk in drive A.
    b. Enter this command:

        A>FORMAT

        DOS will respond:

        ```
        Insert new diskette for drive A: and strike any key
        when ready_
        ```

    c. Put a blank disk in drive A. The FORMAT program will erase any data on the diskette you use; so be sure your disk doesn't contain any valuable data.
    d. Hit any character key. You'll see this message:

        ```
        Formatting . . . _
        ```

        You'll also hear the disk drive working. Then you should see this message:

        ```
        Formatting . . . Format complete

              160256 bytes total disk space
              160256 bytes available on disk

        Format another (Y/N)?_
        ```

        If you have two-sided drives, the number of bytes will be 322,560. If any other message appears, start the process over with another blank disk. You'll learn to handle formatting problems in the next chapter.
    e. Type an N. Do not press Enter. DOS will read the N immediately and terminate the FORMAT program.
    f. Remove the formatted disk from drive A. Put a label on it and mark the label in some way to indicate that the disk is formatted. (We put a small "f" in the upper right corner. Any symbol at all will do, as long as you remember what it is.)
    g. Put the disk back in drive A.

2. Now create several new files on the blank disk by copying from the console to the disk drive. Create as many files as you want, each containing at least one file line, but do at least these four:

```
file identifier: FILEA.X
THIS IS FILE A.

file identifier: FILEB.X
THIS IS FILE B.

file identifier: FILEA.Y
THIS IS THE SECOND PART OF FILE A.

file identifier: FILEB.Y
THIS IS THE SECOND PART OF FILE B.
```

Now get a directory of the new disk. Your new files should be listed. Note the dates and times.

3. Make copies of all your files. (Keep the copies on the new disk also.) Call the copies COPYA.X, COPYB.X, COPYA.Y, and COPYB.Y.

4. Change the date and time to January 1, 1999, at 1:00 in the morning.

5. Make another set of copies of the first four files. Call the new copies NEWA.X, NEWB.X, NEWA.Y, and NEWB.Y.

6. Check your disk directory. What date and time were recorded for your NEW*.* files? Make another set of the files with the 1999 date and time. Call the new set JAN99A.X, JAN99B.X, JAN99A.Y, and JAN99B.Y.

7. You should now have at least 16 files on your directory.

8. Concatenate all the files that start with "FILE" into one file called FILE.ALL.

9. Using TYPE, display FILE.ALL on your terminal.

10. Using COPY, print a copy of FILE.ALL.

11. Concatenate all the files starting with "JAN" into JAN99A.Y. Print a copy of JAN99A.Y.

12. Concatenate all the files with extension A into ALL.A and all the files with extension B into ALL.B. Print copies of ALL.A and ALL.B.

13. Erase JAN99A.X from the disk.

14. Erase all the files whose names start with "COPY" from the disk.

15. Continue to practice the ERASE, TYPE, and COPY commands until you feel comfortable with them.

When you feel ready, shut down the system and go on to Chapter Six.

CHAPTER SIX

DOS External Programs

The commands you learned to use in the previous chapters are built into the command processor of DOS. Your system disk also contains various external programs. These external programs can be used to get information about your disks, to prepare new disks, to create files, and for other handy operations.

In this chapter we're going to overview these programs. You probably won't use all of them, but it's a good idea to know what's available. As you use DOS on the job, you'll quickly learn which of these external programs you'll need most. We will also teach you how to use two of the external programs: FORMAT and SYS. In following chapters, you'll learn more details about other external programs.

When you complete this chapter, you will be able to:

- Differentiate between internal and external programs
- Identify the DOS external programs that would be used to perform various functions
- Use the FORMAT program to prepare a new disk
- Use the SYS program to put the DOS system files on a disk
- Interpret error messages resulting from these external commands

OVERVIEW OF THE EXTERNAL PROGRAMS

1.   In the previous chapters you learned to use the DOS internal commands. These are built into the DOS system and are included in the command processor. Whenever DOS is running, those internal commands are present and can be used. Now we're going to look at the DOS external programs. These are programs provided by IBM in addition to the DOS system itself. They are not part of the command processor but are contained in separate files on your system disk. If you copy your system to another disk, the internal commands will be copied but the external ones won't unless you specifically copy them.

(a) Which type of DOS programs are automatically "on" any disk with the DOS system?_____

(b) What type of DOS program might not be included on every DOS system disk?_____

– – – – – – – – – – – –

(a) internal; (b) external

2. The external programs provided with DOS serve several purposes. We'll overview all of them in this chapter. We'll also look at some of the shorter ones in detail.

Each external program is on the disk in the form of a file with extension EXE or COM. It can be run by entering the filename (without the extension) and any required operands. You'll learn what operands are required as you study each program. Here is a directory listing of a DOS disk that contains the standard DOS external programs:

```
A>dir b:
COMMAND   COM      4959    5–07–82   12:00p
FORMAT    COM      3816    5–07–82   12:00p
CHKDSK    COM      1720    5–07–82   12:00p
SYS       COM       605    5–07–82   12:00p
DISKCOPY  COM      2008    5–07–82   12:00p
DISKCOMP  COM      1640    5–07–82   12:00p
COMP      COM      1649    5–07–82   12:00p
EXE2BIN   EXE      1280    5–07–82   12:00p
MODE      COM      2509    5–07–82   12:00p
EDLIN     COM      2392    5–07–82   12:00p
DEBUG     COM      5999    5–07–82   12:00p
LINK      EXE     41856    5–07–82   12:00p
BASIC     COM     11392    5–07–82   12:00p
BASICA    COM     16768    5–07–82   12:00p
```

Which of the programs below can be run from this disk?

_____ (a) TYPE

_____ (b) SUBGEN

_____ (c) DISKCOPY

_____ (d) RENAME

_____ (e) SYS

_____ (f) EDLIN

— — — — — — — — — —

a, c, d, e, f (a and d are internal and available on every DOS disk, b—SUBGEN—is not on the disk)

3. The EDLIN program is the DOS text editor. You use it to make new files or change old ones. EDLIN is concerned with ASCII, not binary, files. Typical ASCII files might be correspondence, a chapter in a book, a mailing list, or a source program written in a language other than BASIC.

To use EDLIN you enter a command in this format:

EDLIN *file-identifier*

If the file you specify exists, EDLIN will let you change it or add to it. If the file doesn't exist, EDLIN will create a directory entry and let you put information in the file.

Suppose a disk contains only these files: EDLIN.COM, PROG1.ASM, and PROG1.TEX.

(a) What can you do with PROG1.TEX after you enter the command shown below?

A>EDLIN PROG1.TEX

_____

(b) What command will let you create a file called TWO.TRY?

_____

(c) What command will let you modify the ASM file?

_____

— — — — — — — — — —

(a) change it or add to it; (b) EDLIN TWO.TRY (c) EDLIN PROG1.ASM

4. DISKCOPY is used to copy an entire disk rather than individual files. We do this when we want to make a backup copy of a disk for safety's sake. For example, one of the first things you should do is back up your DOS disk. (We walked you through this process in Chapter One.) Then if something happens to one disk, you still have an operating system and don't have to purchase another copy.

(a)   If you want to copy a whole disk, what program do you use?

_____

(b)   If you want to copy one file, what program do you use?

_____

(c)   Suppose you pay $50 for a new STARSHOT game for your computer. What's one of the first things you should do with it—before trying out your new game—if the game's copyright doesn't forbid it?

_____

_____

– – – – – – – – – –

(a) DISKCOPY; (b) COPY; (c) make a backup copy

5.   COMP and DISKCOMP are used to make comparisons. COMP compares two files and tells you if they are the same or different. DISKCOMP compares two disks in the same fashion. These two programs should be used immediately after copy operations to validate the copies. Copying doesn't always work perfectly; so it can be important to check, although many users don't bother. If COMP or DISKCOMP identifies any differences, you can repeat the copy operation.

(a)   Suppose you use COPY to copy a file from drive A to drive B. What's the next program you should use if you want to validate the copy?

_____

(b)   Suppose you use DISKCOPY to copy a disk from drive A to drive B. What's the next program you should use if you want to validate the copy?

_____

– – – – – – – – – –

(a) COMP; (b) DISKCOMP

6.   Before a blank disk can be used in the Personal Computer, it must be formatted (we walked you through this process in Chapter Five). Formatting involves several operations. The disk is checked for any defective tracks, and if any are found, they're made note of so the computer won't try to use them. The directory is prepared. The boot record and File Allocation Table are placed on the disk. If you specify it, the DOS system files are also copied onto the disk (not the external files).

The FORMAT program is used to format a disk. The DISKCOPY program will also format an unformatted disk before it makes the backup copy.

(a) Before you can use any blank disk, what must you do to it?_____

Name two different programs to accomplish that. _____

(b) Which of the following will the FORMAT program do?

_____ A. Prepare directory for disk

_____ B. Put boot record and File Allocation Table on disk

_____ C. Mark defective tracks

_____ D. Put IBMDOS, COMMAND, and IBMBIO on the disk

_____ E. Put the external program files on the disk

(c) True or false? If FORMAT finds a defective track, the disk is rejected and you have to throw it out. _____

— — — — — — — — — —

(a) format it, FORMAT and DISKCOPY; (b) A, B, C, and D; (c) false—FORMAT notes the defective tracks but the rest of the disk can be used

7. CHDSK will give you a status report for a disk and internal memory. The status report looks something like this:

```
160256  bytes total disk space
  8704  bytes in 2 hidden files
  5120  bytes in 1 user files
146432  bytes available on disk
 65536  bytes total memory
 53136  bytes free
```

Notice that the disk in this example has 146K bytes available.

Suppose you have copied 40 files onto a disk and you want to see if you can put an 83K file on. What command will tell you how much space you have left on the disk?_____

— — — — — — — — — —

CHKDSK

8. The mode program adjusts the output mode of the printer. The Personal Computer assumes your printer prints 80 characters per line and 6 lines per inch. If you want to use a different format, you use the MODE program to tell DOS what format to use.

The MODE command is also used to adjust your color monitor. It is not used for the monochrome display.

A third MODE function allows you to establish the characteristics (speed, etc.) of an auxiliary device.

In which of the following cases would you use MODE?

_____ (a) You want to print 80 characters per line, 6 lines per inch.

_____ (b) You want to print 132 characters per line, 8 lines per inch.

_____ (c) You want to adjust the format of your monochrome display.

_____ (d) You want to adjust the format of your color monitor.

_____ (e) You want to transmit data to an auxiliary output device at 960 characters per second.

_____ _____ _____ _____ _____ _____ _____ _____ _____

b, d, and e

9. Sometimes when you buy a program, the disk has been set up for the DOS system files, but they are not on it. The SYS program copies the system files (IBMBIO, IBMDOS, and COMMAND) in that situation.

Why use SYS instead of FORMAT or COPY? FORMAT would erase the program you just paid for in the process of looking for bad sectors. COPY will not copy the system files.

(a) Suppose you want to place the DOS system onto a new blank disk. What program would you use?_____

(b) Suppose you want to copy the DOS external programs onto a disk in drive B. What program would you use?_____

(c) Suppose you want to copy the DOS system files onto a disk that already contains other data. What program would you use?_____

_____ _____ _____ _____ _____ _____ _____ _____

(a) FORMAT; (b) COPY; (c) SYS

PROGRAM-RELATED EXTERNAL PROGRAMS

Three of the external programs are used when you are writing your own programs for the Personal Computer—LINK, EXE2BIN, and DEBUG. We won't teach you how to use these programs in detail, but we will briefly overview what each one does.

10. Programs written in languages such as COBOL and FORTRAN must be translated into the machine's own language before the machine can execute them. After being translated, they must go through another step, called linkage editing. This step brings together parts of the program that have been developed separately.

LINK is the name of the linkage editor for the Personal Computer. It produces an EXE file.

If you won't be writing your own external programs, you'll never use LINK. You don't need to link programs that you buy commercially; they will already be linked. You also don't need to link BASIC programs; the BASIC system translates programs as it executes them.

(a) Which of the following types of programs must you link edit with LINK?

_____ A. Internal programs

_____ B. DOS external programs

_____ C. External programs that you write in COBOL or FORTRAN

_____ D. External programs that you buy

_____ E. External programs that you write in BASIC

(b) What type of program file does LINK create—EXE or COM?

_____

————————————

(a) C; (b) EXE

11. EXE files are not the most efficient type of program files. COM files are faster and take up less room. The EXE2BIN program converts an EXE file to a BIN file, which is very much like a COM file.

Suppose you write a program in COBOL, called SORTER.COB. After translation, it is called SORTER.REL.

(a)   What will it be called after you run it through LINK?

_____

(b)   How can you convert it to a COM-style program?

_____

(c)   What will its name be after you do that?

_____

_ _ _ _ _ _ _ _ _ _

(a) SORTER.EXE; (b) use EXE2BIN; (c) SORTER.BIN

12.   The DEBUG program is used to find errors in a program. (In program slang a "bug" is an error.) The DEBUG program makes available many commands that are helpful in tracking down and correcting errors.

Suppose you wrote your own progam and it doesn't work properly. What DOS external program can help you locate the problem?_____

_ _ _ _ _ _ _ _ _ _

DEBUG

13.   Match these three programs with their functions.

_____ (a)   EXE2BIN
_____ (b)   LINK
_____ (c)   DEBUG

1.   Edits a program and creates an EXE file
2.   Assists in tracking down and correcting program errors
3.   Converts a BASIC program into a COM file
4.   Converts an EXE file to a more efficient format

_ _ _ _ _ _ _ _ _ _

(a) 4; (b) 1; (c) 2

THE FORMAT PROGRAM

Now that we have overviewed all of the external programs, we'll take a more detailed look at all the ones you will use frequently, beginning with FORMAT.

14.   The FORMAT program formats a disk. You cannot use a disk with the Personal Computer until it has been formatted. You can also reformat a disk at any time. Reformatting erases all the data on the disk.
  Here is what the FORMAT program does:

- Sets the disk up in the format used by the Personal Computer
- Looks for and marks any defective tracks
- Initializes the disk with the boot record, a directory, and the File Allocation Table
- Optionally, copies the DOS system files—IBMBIO.COM, IBMDOS.COM, and COMMAND.COM—onto the disk
- Issues a status report showing the amount of space available on the disk for new files

(a)   Suppose you buy a new box of disks. What program would you use to prepare them for the Personal Computer?_____

(b)   Suppose you have a disk of important data that has been giving you trouble and you suspect it has developed a bad sector. Should you use the FORMAT program to find out if it has any bad sectors?_____

      Why?_____

— — — — — — — — — —

(a) FORMAT; (b) no; FORMAT will erase all the data from the disk (first, COPY the important data to another disk, and *then* you can FORMAT the troublesome disk)

15.   To format a disk without using any of the options, you can simply enter this command:

      FORMAT d:

  If you don't enter a drivename, you will be told to put the target disk in the default drive. If you specify the drivename, you will be told to put the target disk in the specified drive. Don't worry—FORMAT won't affect the disk containing the FORMAT.COM file. It always gives you a chance to install the target disk in the specified drive before it begins erasing that disk. The message looks like this:

```
Insert new diskette for drive x
and strike any key when ready_
```

After you do so, and hit any character key, you will get this message:

```
Formatting . . .
```

You will hear the disk drive working. When the operation is complete, you will see this message:

```
Formatting . . . Format complete
        xxxxxxx bytes total disk space
        yyyyyyy bytes in bad sectors
        zzzzzzz bytes available on disk
```

The last three lines give the status of the disk. The "bad sectors" line will be displayed only if some bad sectors were found.

The FORMAT program then asks you:

```
Format another? (Y/N)?_
```

If you do want to format another disk, type the letter Y and the FORMAT program will be repeated. If you don't want to format another disk, type the letter N and the command prompt will be displayed. Don't press Enter after you type the Y or N. (If you do, DOS will interpret the Enter as a "bad" command.)

(a) Code a command to format a disk on the A drive.

A>_____

(b) Code a command to format a disk on the B drive.

A>_____

Suppose you get the following message:

```
Formatting . . . Format complete
        160256 bytes total disk space
        160256 bytes available on disk
Format another? (Y/N)_
```

(c) How many bad sectors are on the disk?_____

(d) Suppose you want to format another disk. What do you type?_____

(e) Suppose you don't want to format another disk. What do you type?_____

(f) Do you press Enter after you type Y or N?_____

—————————————

(a) A>FORMAT or FORMAT A: (b) A>FORMAT B: (c) none; (d) Y (e) N (f) no

16.   Sometimes you want to be able to boot with the disk you're formatting. Then you should make sure the DOS system files are copied into the system tracks. The boot record is put on every formatted disk automatically, but IBMBIO.COM, IBMDOS.COM, and COMMAND.COM are not. To cause FOR-MAT to put those system files on the disk, you use the /S option as in:

```
A>FORMAT/S B:
A>FORMAT B:/S
A>FORMAT /S B:
A>FORMAT B: /S
A>FORMAT /SB:
```

The message you get back from the FORMAT program will look something like this:

```
Formatting . . . Format complete
System Transferred
        160256 bytes total disk space
        13824  bytes used by system
        486     bytes in bad sector
        145946 bytes available on disk
Format another? (Y/N)?_
```

(a) Code a command to format the disk in the A drive so it can be used for booting.

A>_____

(b) Code a command to format the disk in the B drive so it can be used for booting.

A>_____

—————————————

We won't show you all the possible variations of correct answers. You know the /S can go anywhere after the word FORMAT.
(a) A>FORMAT/S (b) A>FORMAT/S B:

17.   By default, the FORMAT program always formats a disk for the drive it's in. Thus, if it's in a single-sided drive, FORMAT prepares it to be used in a single-sided drive. If it's in a double-sided drive, FORMAT prepares it to be used in a double-sided drive.

Disks in single-sided format can be used in double-sided drives. But disks in double-sided format cannot be used in single-sided drives. If you have a double-sided drive, you may want to prepare some disks to be used in single-sided drive. (You may want to copy some data to send to a friend who has single-sided drives.) You can do this with the /1 option, as in:

        A>FORMAT/1
        A>FORMAT /1
        A>FORMAT B:/1
        A>FORMAT B: /1

A disk formatted with the /1 option can be used in single- or double-sided drives; only the first side (160K) is available. You can use the /1 option in conjunction with the /S option.

For the following questions, assume that your A drive is single-sided and your B drive is double-sided.

(a) Code a command to prepare a disk in double-sided format.

    A>_____

(b) Code a command to format a disk on drive B so that it can be used in either drive.

    A>_____

(c) Change the above command so that the disk is bootable.

    A>_____

— — — — — — — — — —

(a) A>FORMAT B: (you have to use drive B to get the double-sided format); (b) A>FORMAT/1 B: (c) A>FORMAT/S/1 B:

18. Here are some of the error messages you can get from FORMAT.

    `Attempted write-protect violation`

You'll get this message if you try to format a write-protected disk.

    `Track 0 bad, disk unusable`
    `Format failure`

FORMAT will work around any bad track except track 0. Since the system information—the boot record, the directory, and the File Allocation Table—must be put on track 0, this track must be good or the whole disk is rejected. If you get this message, throw out the disk, or return it and try to get your money back.

    Disk unsuitable for system disk

This problem crops up only when you have specified FORMAT/S. The tracks to receive the system files—IBMBIOS.COM, IBMDOS.COM, and COMMAND.COM—are bad. You could format this disk without /S, but you can't put the system files on it.

    Insert DOS disk in x
    and strike any key when ready

FORMAT *copies* the system files to the new disk. When it's ready to do that, it needs to have a source for the three files. If it can't find a source, it asks you to install one. When you see this message, put any disk containing the system files in the indicated drive.

(a) Which of the following messages means the target disk cannot be formatted and should be discarded?

   _____ A. Attempted write protection violation

   _____ B. Track 0 bad, disk unusable

   _____ C. Disk unsuitable for system disk

(b) Which of the following messages can result only from a FORMAT/S operation?

   _____ A. Insert DOS disk in x and strike any key when ready

   _____ B. Track 0 bad, disk unusable

   _____ C. Disk unsuitable for system disk

   _____ D. Attempted write protect violation

(c) How does FORMAT get the system files to put on a formatted disk?

   _____ A. It copies them from ROM

   _____ B. They're included in the FORMAT program

   _____ C. It copies them from another disk

— — — — — — — — — —

(a) B; (b) A, C; (c) C

THE SYS COMMAND

19. You've learned how to put the system files on a new disk with FORMAT/S. But FORMAT erases and reformats a disk. How do you put the system files on a disk that you don't want to erase? You can't use COPY because it won't copy IBMBIO.COM and IBMDOS.COM.

The correct command is SYS. It exists specifically to copy the system files from one disk to another. The default drive must contain the files to be copied. The SYS.COM file must also be available. The only operand you can specify is the destination drive. To copy the system files from drive A to drive B, you would enter:

    A>SYS B:

You can't use SYS to put the system files on a disk that wasn't formatted with /S to begin with; such a disk would not have room for the system files. The primary use of SYS is to put your system files on a prerecorded disk when the documentation for that disk tells you to do so.

(a) Select the true statements below.

    _____ A. SYS copies the system files from the default drive to the specified drive.

    _____ B. SYS can be used when you formatted a disk without the /S option.

    _____ C. Two ways to copy system files from A: to B: are SYS and COPY.

    _____ D. SYS will put your system files on a prerecorded disk (if room has been left for them).

(b) Code a command to copy the system files from A: to B:. Assume the disk in A contains the system files and SYS.COM.

    A>_____

(c) What's wrong with this command: SYS B: A: _____

_____

_____

_ _ _ _ _ _ _ _ _ _

(a) A, D; (b) A>SYS B:(c) you can specify only one drivename with SYS—the destination drive.

20. Here are three messages you haven't seen before.

```
Invalid parameter
```

This message means you have used an invalid drivename. Perhaps you left out the colon or typed a wrong letter.

```
No room for system on destination disk
```

This message means that the disk wasn't formatted for the system files in the first place. You cannot put the system files on this disk.

```
Incompatible system size
```

The target disk has some room for the system files, but not enough. It must have been formatted by and for a smaller system. You can't put your system files on this disk.

In either of the above cases, how could you create a disk containing the appropriate system files *plus* the data files from the disk that won't work with SYS?

_____

_____

_____

– – – – – – – – – – –

Use FORMAT/S to set up a blank disk with the correct system files, and then use COPY to transfer the files to the system disk.

Chapter Six Self-Test

1. Label each of the following DOS programs as EXTERNAL or INTERNAL.

   a. COPY _____ d. TYPE _____

   b. DISKCOPY _____ e. COMP _____

   c. FORMAT _____ f. ERASE _____

2. Which of the following statements are true? (Choose more than one.)
   a. To run an external program, the program file must be available on disk when you enter the command.
   b. To run an internal program, the program file must be available on disk when you enter the command.
   c. Anytime DOS is running, you can use the external programs; they don't need to be available on disk.
   d. Anytime DOS is running, you can use the internal programs; they don't need to be available on disk.

3. Suppose your disk directory looks like this:

```
COMMAND    COM    4959     5–07–82    12:00p
FORMAT     COM    3816     5–07–82    12:00p
SYS        COM     605     5–07–82    12:00p
FILEONE           2816    10–15–83     1:15p
FILETWO           2904    10–16–83     9:18a
```

Which of the following commands will DOS run?
a. TYPE
b. CHKDSK
c. SYS
d. COPY
e. COMP
f. DATE

4. Which DOS programs would you use for the following functions?

a. Copy an entire disk on a track-by-track basis. _____

b. Copy an entire disk on a file-by-file basis. _____

c. Change (edit) a text file. _____

d. Find out how many bytes remain available on a disk. _____

e. Prepare a disk to be used by DOS. _____

f. Compare two disks. _____

g. Compare two files. _____

h. Adjust the output mode of your printer. _____

i. Copy the DOS system files onto a disk without erasing the disk. _____

j. Link edit a program file. _____

k. Convert an EXE file into a BIN file. _____

l. Find and correct errors in a program. _____

5. Code commands for the following functions.

a. Prepare the new disk in drive B to be used by DOS. Include the system files on it.

    A>_____

b. Prepare the new disk in drive A to be used by DOS. Even though drive A is double-sided, prepare the disk for use in a single-sided drive.

    A>_____

c. Copy the system files from A to B. Room has been left for them on the disk in B.

    A>_____

6. Suppose you have the following interaction:

```
A>SYS B:
No room for system on destination disk
A>_
```

What's wrong?_____

7. Which of the following statements is true?

    a. If FORMAT locates bad sectors anywhere on a disk, the disk is rejected.

    b. FORMAT rejects a disk if the boot sector is defective, but otherwise it just marks bad sectors so they won't be used for file data.

    c. FORMAT marks bad sectors, but never completely rejects a disk.

    d. You can choose how you want FORMAT to handle bad sectors.

8. True or false? FORMAT puts the boot record on every disk. _____

9. True or false? FORMAT erases a disk in the process of formatting it. _____

10. True or false? FORMAT always formats a disk for a double-sided drive unless told to do otherwise. _____

Self-Test Answer Key

1. a. Internal   d. Internal
    b. External   e. External
    c. External   f. Internal

2. a and d

3. a, c, d, f

4. a. DISKCOPY   g. COMP
    b. COPY   h. MODE
    c. EDLIN   i. SYS
    d. CHKDSK   j. LINK
    e. FORMAT   k. EXE2BIN
    f. DISKCOMP   l. DEBUG

5. a. A>FORMAT/S B:
    b. A>FORMAT1
    c. A>SYS B:

6. The disk was not formatted with the /S option.

7. b

8. True

9. True

10. False—it formats the disk for the drive it's in.

Suggested Machine Exercise

1. Start up the system.

2. Format a few disks. (Be sure to mark your formatted disks in some way.) Format some with the system and some without. Try booting with these disks.

3. Try using SYS to copy the system files from one disk to another.

4. Keep practicing these commands until you feel comfortable with them. Then shut down your system and go on to Chapter Seven.

CHAPTER SEVEN

More External Programs

This chapter takes a closer look at these external programs: DISKCOPY, DISKCOMP, COMP, CHKDSK, and MODE. We'll show you how to use each program and how to handle some of the error messages you might encounter.

When you complete this chapter, you'll be able to:

- Use the DISKCOPY program to make a copy of a disk
- State when to use DISKCOPY and when to use COPY
- Use the DISKCOMP program to compare two disks
- Use the COMP program to compare two files
- Use the CHKDSK program to get a status report on a disk
- Use the MODE program to change output modes
- Identify other functions of the MODE program
- Interpret error messages resulting from these external commands

THE DISKCOPY COMMAND

1. DISKCOPY is used to make a complete copy of a disk. DISKCOPY does not copy first file A, then file B, and so on. It simply starts with the first track and copies to the last track without regard to files, bad sectors, and the like. When done, the new disk is exactly the same (supposedly) as the source disk.

Let's compare DISKCOPY with COPY B:*.*. DISKCOPY will copy the system track as well as the file tracks. With DISKCOPY, if the source disk contained the system files, the new disk would also. With COPY, the system track and the system files are never copied.

COPY copies on a file-by-file basis; it pays attention to the condition of the receiving disk. If the disk has existing files or bad sectors, the new files are fit in where there is room for them. DISKCOPY obliterates any previous information on the target disk. When done, the target disk is a true copy of the source disk.

(a) Label each of the following as DISKCOPY or COPY.

    A. Copies on a file-by-file basis _____

    B. Copies tracks without regard to files _____

    C. Copies system files _____

    D. Copies bad tracks _____

    E. Erases all previous information on target disk _____

    F. Formats as it copies _____

(b) Suppose you want to make a vault copy of the disk on A. You know that the disk on A contains some bad tracks and the disk on B doesn't. Should you use COPY or DISKCOPY?_____

(c) Suppose you want to make a vault copy of the disk on A. You know that the source disk is free of bad tracks but the disk on B has at least one bad track.

Should you use COPY or DISKCOPY?_____

(d) Suppose you want to make a vault copy of the disk on A. Neither the source nor the target disk has any bad tracks. Should you use COPY or DISKCOPY?

_____

(e) Suppose you want to make a vault copy of the disk on A. The target disk has some information on it, which should not be erased. Should you use COPY or DISKCOPY?_____

— — — — — — — — — —

(a)A—COPY; B—DISKCOPY; C—DISKCOPY; D—DISKCOPY; E-DISKCOPY; F—DISKCOPY;(b)COPY (DISKCOPY would copy the bad tracks) (c) COPY (DISKCOPY would try to write on the bad track); (d) DISKCOPY (it's faster); (e) COPY (DISKCOPY would erase the existing information)

2. The format of the DISKCOPY command is:

    DISKCOPY d: d:

The drivenames are optional. If you leave them off, DOS assumes you want to use the default drive for both disks. You will be told when to put the source disk in and when to put the target disk in. You'll have to switch disks several times.
    To copy from drive A to drive B, use this command:

    DISKCOPY A: B:

    If you specify only one drivename, it is assumed to be the source drive. The default drive is used as the target drive.

To copy from a double-sided disk to a single-sided one, use the /1 parameter, as in DISKCOPY A: B:/1. (DOS copies as much as it can to the single-sided disk.)

(a)   Match the equivalent statements below.

    ____ A.   A>DISKCOPY   1.   A>DISKCOPY B: B:

    ____ B.   B>DISKCOPY   2.   B>DISKCOPY A:

                                               3.   B>DISKCOPY A: B:

    ____ C.   A>DISKCOPY B: A: 4.   A>DISKCOPY A: A:

    ____ D.   A>DISKCOPY A: B: 5.   A>COPY *.* B:

                                             6.   A>DISKCOPY A:

                                             7.   B>COPY *.* A:

                                             8.   A>DISKCOPY B:

(b)   Code a command to make a copy of the disk on drive A. Put the copy on drive B.

    A>_____

(c)   Code a command to make a copy of one side only of the disk in drive A. Keep the copy in drive A.

    A>_____

— — — — — — — — — — —

(a) A—4, 6; B—1; C—8; D—2, 3; (b) A>DISKCOPY A: B: (c) DISKCOPY/1

3.   A successful two-drive DISKCOPY interaction looks like this:

```
A>DISKCOPY A: B:
Insert source diskette in drive A:
Insert target diskette in drive B:
Strike any key when ready
Copying 1 side(s)
Copy complete
Copy another (Y/N)?N
A>
```

If the target disk is unformatted, you will also see the message "Formatting while copying."

Suppose you want to copy a new game disk you have just bought. Remember that DISKCOPY is an external program, so you must start with a disk containing the DISKCOPY.COM file. Therefore, three disks are involved. We'll call them the DOS disk (which contains DISKCOPY.COM), the game disk, and the target disk.

(a) Before you enter the DISKCOPY command, what disk would you put in drive A?_____

Now you enter the command A>DISKCOPY A: B: The system responds:

```
Insert source diskette in drive A:
Insert target diskette in drive B:
Strike any key when ready_
```

(b) Which disk do you put in drive A?_____

(c) Which disk do you put in drive B?_____

— — — — — — — — — — —

(a) DOS; (b) game; (c) target

4.   Let's look at some of the error messages involved with DISKCOPY. Here are some old familiar ones:

```
Not ready error reading (or writing) drive x
Correct, then strike any key_
or
Abort, Retry, Ignore?_
```

```
Invalid parameter
```

You should know how to handle these. Below are some messages you've not seen before.

```
Target diskette write protected
Correct, then strike any key
```

This should be self-explanatory.

```
Incompatible drive types
```

The source drive is two-sided, and the target drive is single-sided. The target disk will not have usable data; so don't try to rescue it. You can redo the copy using DISKCOPY/1.

```
Unrecoverable format error on target
Target diskette unusable

Unrecoverable read error on source.
Track xx, side x
Target disk may be unusable

Unrecoverable write (or verify) error on target
Track xx, side x
Target disk may be unusable
```

In all the above cases, something went wrong with the copy. The data on the target disk should not be used.

Which of the following statements is true?

_____ (a) Whenever DOS says, "Target disk unusable" or "Target disk may be unusable," you should avoid trying to use the target disk for anything.

_____ (b) You can copy from a two-sided drive to a one-sided drive. DOS automatically converts the data to the right format.

— — — — — — — — — —

(a) is true

DISKCOMP AND COMP

5. No computer copying operation is 100 percent reliable. Slight variations in electricity, read/write head tolerances, and the like can produce occasional errors. DOS gives you the opportunity to double-check every copy you make with the DISKCOMP and COMP commands. DISKCOMP compares two disks and COMP compares two files. Differences, if any, are reported on the monitor. You may want to use DISKCOMP after DISKCOPY and COMP after COPY if you have not used /V with the COPY command.

The format of the DISKCOMP command is identical to that of DISKCOPY, except for the command name itself. You can specify none, one, or two drivenames. You can specify /1 to limit the target disk to the first side. Here is a printout of a DISKCOMP interaction:

```
A>DISKCOMP A: B:
Insert first diskette in drive A:
Insert second diskette in drive B:
Strike any key when ready
Comparing 1 side(s)
Diskettes compare ok
Compare more diskettes (Y/N)?N
```

To compare two files, you enter COMP followed by the two file names, as in:

```
COMP TEACT.A B:TEACT.A

Insert diskette(s) with files to compare and strike any key
when ready

Files compare ok

Compare more files (Y/N)?N
```

If you leave out the file names, COMP will ask for them, like this:

```
Enter primary file name
TEACT.A
Enter 2nd file name or drive id
B:
Insert diskette(s) with files to compare and strike any key
when ready

Files compare ok

Compare more files (Y/N)?N
```

The above interaction also demonstrates that you can omit the second file-name if it's the same as the first.

You can use global file identifiers if you wish, but only the first two files will be compared.

(a) Code a command to compare two disks—one on A and one on B.

A>_____

(b) Which disk should be in drive A when you enter the above command?

_____

(c) Code a command to compare the double-sided disk in drive A with the single-sided disk in drive B.

A>_____

(d) Code a command to compare LONG and SHORT. Both files are on drive A.

A>_____

(e) Code a command to compare STONES on drive A with a file of the same name on drive B.

A>_____

(f)   Can you code one command to compare all the files with extension DOC on drive A to like-named files on drive B?_____ If so, show the command.

A>_____

(g)   Which of the following commands are not legitimate?

_____ A.   A>COMP

_____ B.   A>DISKCOMP

_____ C.   B>COMP A:

_____ D.   A>DISKCOMP A:

_____ E.   A>DISKCOMP *.*

_____ F.   A>COMP *.* B:

_____ G.   A>COMP QUIZ2

_____ H.   A>COMP QUIZ* TEST*

_ _ _ _ _ _ _ _ _ _ _

(a) A>DISKCOMP A: B: *or* A>DISKCOMP B: (b) the disk containing DISKCOMP.COM; (c) A>DISKCOMP/1 A: B: (d) A>COMP LONG SHORT (e) A>COMP STONES B: (f) no—only two files can be compared with each command; (g) E—only drivenames can be used with DISKCOMP; G—since the second drive defaults to A, you're trying to compare A:QUIZ2 to A:QUIZ2

6.   You've seen examples of successful comparisons. Now let's look at some other DISKCOMP and COMP messages.

Suppose the comparison identifies one or more mistakes:

```
COMP TEACT.A TEACT.B

Insert diskette(s) with files to compare and strike any key
when ready

Compare error at offset C
File 1 = 61
File 2 = 62
```

Suppose the two files you try to compare have different sizes recorded in the directory. COMP won't even try to compare them:

```
Insert diskette(s) with files to compare and strike any key
when ready

Files are different sizes

Compare more files (Y/N)?N
```

Suppose the two items being compared are very different. Both COMP and DISKCOMP give up after 10 mistakes are found:

```
Insert diskette(s) with files to compare and strike any key
when ready

Compare error at offset 0
File 1 = 74
File 2 = 6E

Compare error at offset 1
File 1 = 68
File 2 = 6F

Compare error at offset 2
File 1 = 69
File 2 = 77

Compare error at offset 3
File 1 = 73
File 2 = 20

Compare error at offset 4
File 1 = 20
File 2 = 77

Compare error at offset 5
File 1 = 69
File 2 = 65

Compare error at offset 6
File 1 = 73
File 2 = 27
```

```
Compare error at offset 7
File 1 = 20
File 2 = 6C

Compare error at offset 8
File 1 = 74
File 2 = 6C

Compare error at offset 9
File 1 = 68
File 2 = 20

10 Mismatches – aborting compare

Compare more files (Y/N)?N
A>
```

You might also encounter the following messages:

```
EOF mark not found
```

This is not really an error as long as the files are program files. Recall that ASCII files end with ˆZ (the EOF mark) and program files don't.

```
File n empty
```

The indicated files contains no data. Something must have gone wrong during the copy process.

```
File n not found
```

The indicated file is not on the disk. Double-check your command.

You might also see some of the same error messages we have discussed before, such as "Incompatible drive types."

Which of the following statements are true?

_____ (a) "EOF mark not found" means something is wrong with one or both of the files.

_____ (b) DISKCOMP and COMP both give up after ten mismatches.

_____ (c) COMP won't even try to compare two files with different sizes.

————————————

(b) and (c) are true

THE CHKDSK COMMAND

7. When you run FORMAT, you get a handy status report of the formatted disk. You can get a similar report, containing even more information, from the CHKDSK command. Here are some typical CHKDSK interactions:

```
A>CHKDSK A:

   160256   bytes total disk space
     8704   bytes in 2 hidden files
   143360   bytes in 32 user files
     8192   bytes available on disk

    65536   bytes total memory
    53136   bytes free
```

This report of the default drive shows a typical DOS disk. The two "hidden" files are IBMBIO.COM and IBMDOS.COM which are never included in disk directories. Note that we have room for 8192 more bytes on this disk. The report also gives us the status of memory; there are 53,136 bytes free in memory.

Now let's look at another disk, this time on drive B:

```
A>CHKDSK B:

   160256   bytes total disk space
    19456   bytes in 2 user files
   140800   bytes available on disk

    65536   bytes total memory
    53136   bytes free
```

Here we have a disk with only two user files (so far) and 140,800 bytes of free space. Note that memory hasn't changed.

Now let's look at a disk that has a few problems.

```
A>CHKDSK B:
Allocation error for file SUPER ONG
Allocation error for file CONTROLZ
Allocation error for file WHAT A
Allocation error for file WHAT B
Allocation error for file ABC

   160256   bytes total disk space
    31744   bytes in 10 user files
   128512   bytes available on disk

    65536   bytes total memory
    53136   bytes free
```

The directory on this disk was destroyed by hitting "Retry" at the wrong time. (We warned you about this in Chapter Five.) About the only way to rescue this situation is to reformat the disk and start over. This is a good demonstration of why we faithfully make backup copies of all important disks.

Here are two situations in which there is no data on the disk:

```
A>CHKDSK B:
Diskette not initialized

A>CHKDSK B:
   160256   bytes total disk space
   160256   bytes available on disk

    65536   bytes total memory
    53136   bytes free
```

In the first case, the disk has never been formatted. In the second case, the disk has been formatted but contains no files. Thus, all 160,256 bytes are available.

(a) Code a command to get a status report of the disk in drive A.

A>_____

(b) Code a command to get a status report of the disk in drive B.

A>_____

(c) Which of the following is true?

_____ A. After you enter the CHKDSK command, DOS asks you to install the target disk on the specified drive.

_____ B. DOS assumes the target disk is already installed and checks it immediately after you enter the CHKDSK command.

(d) Suppose you have the following interaction:

```
A>CHKDSK A:

   160256   bytes total in disk space
     8704   bytes in 2 hidden files
   101888   bytes in 14 user files
    49664   bytes available on disk

    65536   bytes total memory
    53136   bytes free
```

What are the two hidden files?

_____

_____

(a) A>CHKDSK or CHKDSK A: (b) A>CHKDSK B: (c) B; (d) IBMBIO.COM and IBMDOS.COM

THE MODE COMMAND

8. MODE is used to control the format of an output device. We'll start by showing you how to change printer modes. DOS will print either 80 or 132 characters per line and either six or eight lines per inch. Unless instructed otherwise, it will print 80 characters per line and six lines per inch. This is a very readable format. Some printers can print up to 132 characters per line, however. The standard printer for the Personal Computer can do so by printing smaller characters. Here's a sample interaction:

```
B>MODE LPT1: 132

Resident portion of MODE loaded

LPT1: not redirected.

LPT1: set for 132

A>DIR
COMMAND   COM    4959  5-07-82   12:00p
FORMAT    COM    3816  5-07-82   12:00p
CHKDSK    COM    1720  5-07-82   12:00p
SYS       COM     605  5-07-82   12:00p
DISKCOPY  COM    2008  5-07-82   12:00p
DISCOMP   COM    1640  5-07-82   12:00p
COMP      COM    1649  5-07-82   12:00p
EXE2BIN   EXE    1280  5-07-82   12:00p
MODE      COM    2509  5-07-82   12:00p
EDLIN     COM    2392  5-07-82   12:00p
DEBUG     COM    5999  5-07-82   12:00p
LINK      EXE   41856  5-07-82   12:00p
BASIC     COM   11392  5-07-82   12:00p
BASICA    COM   16768  5-07-82   12:00p
ART       BAS    1920  5-07-82   12:00p
```

The MODE command sets the print line to 132 characters. The sample directory shows you how much smaller the print is. (We'll explain the message about LPT1: not redirected in the next frame.)

The same printer can also print at eight lines per inch. Here's a sample interaction:

```
A>MODE LPT1: 132,8

LPT1: not redirected.

LPT1: set for 132

Printer lines per inch set

A>DIR
COMMAND    COM    4959   5-07-82   12:00p
FORMAT     COM    3816   5-07-82   12:00p
CHKDSK     COM    1720   5-07-82   12:00p
SYS        COM     605   5-07-82   12:00p
DISKCOPY   COM    2008   5-07-82   12:00p
DISKCOMP   COM    1640   5-07-82   12:00p
COMP       COM    1649   5-07-82   12:00p
EXE2BIN    EXE    1280   5-07-82   12:00p
MODE       COM    2509   5-07-82   12:00p
EDLIN      COM    2392   5-07-82   12:00p
DEBUG      COM    5999   5-07-82   12:00p
LINK       EXE   41856   5-07-82   12:00p
BASIC      COM   11392   5-07-82   12:00p
BASICA     COM   16768   5-07-82   12:00p
ART        BAS    1920   5-07-82   12:00p
SAMPLES    BAS    2432   5-07-82   12:00p
MORTGAGE   BAS    6272   5-07-82   12:00p
COLORBAR   BAS    1536   5-07-82   12:00p
CALENDAR   BAS    3840   5-07-82   12:00p
MUSIC      BAS    8704   5-07-82   12:00p
DONKEY     BAS    3584   5-07-82   12:00p
CIRCLE     BAS    1664   5-07-82   12:00p
PIECHART   BAS    2304   5-07-82   12:00p
SPACE      BAS    1920   5-07-82   12:00p
BALL       BAS    2048   5-07-82   12:00p
PRICRITE   BAS     256   9-01-82   10:16a
            26 File(s)
```

Compare the directory at eight lines per inch to the previous one; you should be able to see the size difference.

If your printer is capable of switching print sizes, you probably will do so only for long print jobs where you want to conserve some paper. For your everyday work, the default mode is usually preferable.

When you code the MODE command to change the print format, keep these rules in mind:

- There must be one, and only one, space after the keyword MODE.
- The first operand indicates the printer: LPT1: If you have more than one printer, you can specify LPT2: or LPT3:.
- You must include the colon (:) after LPT1. (This is different from the COPY command, where the colon is optional.)

- The space after LPT1: is optional.
- The second operand indicates the number of characters per line; it can be 80 or 132.
- If you use the third operand, you must include the comma before it.
- The third operand indicates the number of lines per inch; it can be six or eight.

(a) Code a command to use 132 characters per line on your printer.

A>_____

(b) Code a command to use 132 characters per line and eight lines per inch on your printer.

A>_____

(c) Code a command to use 80 characters per line and eight lines per inch on your printer.

A>_____

(d) Which of the following are *not* correct?

_____ A. A>MODE LPT2 132

_____ B. A>MODE   LPT3:80,8

_____ C. A>MODE LPT1: 80 8

_____ D. A>MODE LPT1: 132,6

_____ E. A>MODE LPT2:100

_____ F. A>MODE LPT3:132,10

— — — — — — — — — —

(a) A>MODE LPT1: 132 (b) A>MODE LPT1: 132,8 (c) A>MODE LPT1: 80,8 (d) A—missing colon; B—too many spaces after MODE; C—missing comma; E—illegal number of characters per line; F—illegal number of lines per inch

9.   There are several other things you can do with the MODE command. We'll tell you what they are, but we won't show you how to use them. If you need to use them, you can look up MODE in your DOS manual.

- You can adjust the display on your color monitor (not your monochrome display), setting it to 40 or 80 characters per line and shifting it right or left so the entire line shows.
- You can adjust a special adapter for communications equipment (if you have one).
- You can tell DOS to use the communications equipment instead of the printer. This one way to send data through the adapter. (When you see the message "LPT1: not redirected," it means you *didn't* do this.)

Which of the following can be adjusted by the MODE command?

_____ (a) Communications equipment

_____ (b) Printer

_____ (c) Monochrome display

_____ (d) Color monitor

_____ (e) Keyboard

_ _ _ _ _ _ _ _ _ _

a, b, and d

Chapter Seven Self-Test

1. Make an exact duplicate of the disk in drive A. The target disk is in drive B. It has not yet been formatted.

   A>_____

2. Make an exact duplicate of the first side only of the disk in drive A. You have only one drive.

   A>_____

3. Make sure the disk you just created in the above command is an exact duplicate of the original.

   A>_____

4. Copy the file named CHAP7EX from drive A to drive B, and verify that it's an exact copy.

   A>_____

   A>_____

5. Get a status report of the disk in drive A.

   A>_____

6. Print at 132 characters per line and eight lines per inch.

   A>_____

7. Suppose you have the following interaction:

   ```
   A>COMPDISK
   Bad command or file name
   ```

   What's wrong?_____

8. Suppose you have the following interaction:

```
160256   bytes total disk space
  8704   bytes in 2 hidden files
142848   bytes in 31 user files
  8704   bytes available on disk
```

What are the "hidden files"?_____

9. Which of the following statements is true?

    a.   COMP and DISKCOMP give up after ten mismatches.
    b.   COMP and DISKCOMP will report every mismatch, no matter how many there are.

10. True or false? COMP won't compare two files with different sizes. _____

11. True or false? DISKCOPY will copy bad sector information. _____

12. True or false? DISKCOPY requires two disk drives. _____

13. What command would you use to align the display on a color TV attached to your Personal Computer?_____

Self-Test Answer Key

1. A>DISKCOPY A: B:

2. A>DISKCOPY/1

3. A>DISKCOMP/1

4. A>COPY CHAP7EX B:
   A>COMP CHAP7EX B:
   or A> COPY /V CHAP7EX B:

5. A>CHKDSK

6. A>MODE LPT1: 132,8

7. There is no program named COMPDISK on drive A. (You probably meant DISKCOMP.)

8. IBMBIO.COM and IBMDOS.COM

9. a

10. True

11. True

12. False—you can do single-drive DISKCOPY operations

13. MODE

Suggested Machine Exercise

1. Start up the system.

2. Make backup copies of any program disks you have, including your DOS disk. (Be sure to properly label every disk.)

3. Verify all your copies (including ones you made in previous chapters) using DISKCOMP and COMP. If you find any mismatches, recopy the file on disk.

4. Use CHKDSK to get a status report of all your disks.

5. Change your printer mode and print some files.

6. Keep practicing these commands until you feel comfortable with them. Then shut down your system and go on to Chapter Eight.

CHAPTER EIGHT
Using the EDLIN Program

The EDLIN program is the DOS editor. You can use EDLIN to type new files and store them on disk. You can also use EDLIN to change existing files. Have you noticed when you create a new file by copying from the console that you can't go back and correct any lines already entered? With EDLIN, you can go back and correct lines.

EDLIN is different from the other DOS programs you have studied. After you enter the EDLIN command, you can enter many special editing commands to control the editor. You interact with EDLIN much as you do with DOS, but on a different level. In this and the next two chapters, you will learn to use all the EDLIN commands.

Not many people use EDLIN. Line editors such as EDLIN are difficult to use in comparison to full screen editors, such as word processors. If you will be using a full screen editor, don't bother learning EDLIN. Skip ahead to Chapter Eleven.

In this chapter, you'll learn to create a file with EDLIN and store it on disk. When you have finished this chapter, you will be able to:

- Initiate EDLIN for a new file
- Use EDLIN's insert level
- Store data lines in memory
- List lines from a file on the console
- Terminate EDLIN

LINE EDITING

1.   EDLIN is a line editor. You use it to create and change files that consist of lines of text data. You can't use EDLIN with binary files, such as COM or EXE files. While you are using EDLIN, you type lines of data at your console, pressing Enter after each line. EDLIN saves the lines in memory. When you're finished, EDLIN can save the file on disk or abandon it, at your command.

If you want to edit an existing file, EDLIN reads it from the disk into memory. You use EDLIN editing commands to make your changes, add lines, delete lines, etc. Then EDLIN can save the changed version on disk, along with the old version.

Which of the following can EDLIN be used for?

_____ (a)   Create a new COM file

_____ (b)   Create a new data file

_____ (c)   Change an existing EXE file

_____ (d)   Change an existing data file

_____ (e)   Change data on the system tracks

— — — — — — — — — —

b, d

2.   EDLIN is a line editor. That means it operates on one line at a time. The data in a file is treated as a series of lines, each ending with a carriage return (↵). A line can be up to 253 characters in length; all the data that appears between two carriage returns constitutes a line.

All the lines that are in memory at one time are automatically numbered, beginning with 1, when you use EDLIN. You'll see the numbers on the console when you use EDLIN; these numbers are not a part of the file and aren't counted in the 253-character line limit. If you add or remove lines, all remaining line numbers are automatically adjusted.

(a)   On what element does EDLIN operate?

_____ A.   A character

_____ B.   A word

_____ C.   A line

_____ D.   A file

(b)   Which of the following could be a valid line in an EDLIN file?

_____ A.   40 characters

_____ B.   80 characters

_____ C.   160 characters

_____ D.   320 characters

(c)   What marks the end of each line in an EDLIN file?_____

(d)   On the terminal, what marks the beginning of each EDLIN line?

_____ A.   Carriage return

_____ B.   Line number

_____ C.   Nothing

—————————

(a) C; (b) A, B, C; (c) carriage return; (d) B

3. As you use EDLIN, one line is always current. EDLIN keeps track of it and displays an asterisk (*) after the line number and before the data line. Here's how it looks:

```
3:  This is a sample section showing
4:*three lines under EDLIN.
5:  The asterisk marks the current line.
```

You can edit or change only the current line. You'll see more about how the current line affects what you do as you continue with this chapter.

(a) What marks the current line in a file being edited under EDLIN?

_____

(b) What line can you edit under EDLIN?

_____ A. Any line at any time

_____ B. The current line

—————————

(a) asterisk or *; (b) B

CREATING A NEW FILE

4. When you are ready to create a file, you must have the EDLIN.COM file on a disk in your machine. You must also have space on one of your disks to hold the new file. *This last is extremely important.* You can lose several hours worth of work if you type it all out and there is no room for it on the disk.

You initiate EDLIN by entering the command EDLIN followed by the filename. Here are some examples:

```
A>EDLIN FILE1.NEW
A>B:EDLIN FILE1.NEW
A>EDLIN B:FILE1.NEW
```

You can see that you use the drivename as needed. When you are creating a new file, you must be sure to use a unique file identifier; otherwise, you won't create a new file. When you issue the EDLIN command for a file, EDLIN looks for an existing file of that name. If it doesn't find one, it creates a file with the name you specified and an extension of $$$. For the first example above, EDLIN allocates a file and assigns it the name FILE1.$$$. Eventually, EDLIN will give this file the extension you specified or erase it, depending on how you terminate EDLIN.

You'll see later what happens when you edit an existing file.

(a) Write a command to create a new file called COPY.DOC.

A>_____

(b) What file name is used on the disk when your command is executed?

_____

(c) Write a command to create a new file named CANCEL.LET and store it on the B drive.

A>_____

— — — — — — — — — —

(a) EDLIN COPY.DOC (b) COPY.$$$; (c) EDLIN B:CANCEL.LET

5. When you enter an EDLIN command and the file you specify doesn't exist, filename.$$$ is created and this is displayed:

```
New file
*_
```

EDLIN is ready to let you create a new file. The asterisk (*) here is not the line pointer indicator; no line numbers are seen. The file doesn't contain any lines yet. When you don't see line numbers, the * tells you that EDLIN expects an EDLIN command.

You can add lines to a file under EDLIN by invoking insert mode, the mode that allows you to enter new lines in a file. You do that with the I command. You simply type I (either upper- or lowercase) and press Enter.

```
New file
*I
        1:*_
```

EDLIN is now in insert mode. You can type data on line 1 (it is the current line, as indicated by the asterisk). When you press Enter, you see this:

```
New file
*I
        1:*This is the first line.
        2:*_
```

Now line 2 is current. Notice that the data remains on the console screen. You can see the results of the last several commands. The current line is indicated by the last line number marked with an asterisk.

(a) What is the current line in the last example above?

_____

(b) Suppose you type "This is the second line." on line 2. How can you add line 3?_____

(c) How can you tell whether an asterisk indicates the current line or that EDLIN is ready for a command?

_____ A. If the * is at the far left of the screen, it indicates the current line.

_____ B. If the * is at the far right of the screen, it indicates the command level.

_____ C. If the asterisk follows a line number, it indicates the current line.

(d) Write a command to allow you to create a new file named PRACTICE.

A>_____

(e) This appears on the screen:

```
New file
*
```

What do you enter to allow you to write lines in the file?

_____

(f) Now this appears:

```
1: *_
```

What do you do to put "Line 1" on the first line and be ready to enter line 2?

_____

— — — — — — — — —

(a) 2; (b) press Enter; (c) C; (d) A>EDLIN PRACTICE (e) I (the command I) (f) type "Line 1" and press Enter

6.   Now suppose the console screen contains this:

```
New line
*I
        1:*This is the first line.
        2:*This is the second line.
        3:*This is the third line.
        4:*_
```

You can continue adding lines or stop.

Suppose you want to stop at three lines. You just press Ctrl-Break. As you know, with other DOS programs Ctrl-Break will terminate the program and return to DOS. When you are in insert mode with EDLIN, however, Ctrl-Break terminates only insert mode and returns you to the EDLIN asterisk prompt. (Ctrl-Z will also do this.) Now the screen contains this:

```
New line
*I
        1:*This is the first line.
        2:*This is the second line.
        3:*This is the third line.
        4:*^C
*_
```

This asterisk tells you EDLIN is ready for a new command. The current line is *after* line 3. If you use I again, you'll get this:

```
*I
        4:*_
```

Suppose the last few lines on your console look like this:

```
        6:*This is the reason that
        7:*DOS is with us today.
        8:*_
```

(a)   How can you terminate insert mode?

_____

(b)   After you terminate insert mode, you see this:

```
        8:*^C
*_
```

What can you enter here? _____

(c)   Suppose you enter I. On what line number will you be able to enter data?

_____

— — — — — — — — — —

(a) Ctrl-Break; (b) any EDLIN command; (c) line 8

7.   When you are in insert mode, you enter lines just like you enter DOS commands. You can use backspace to go back and correct errors, but it erases as it backspaces. You may find it easier to just leave errors in the material and go back and make corrections later. You'll learn in just a bit how to change lines that you have already entered.

You will eventually want to stop editing a file. You may or may not wish to save the result on disk. EDLIN has two separate commands for ending EDLIN, Q and E.

If you don't want to save the new file, you use the Q command to quit the edit session. (You might do this if you discover that you have typed the wrong data.) Here's how it looks:

```
        7:*DOS is with us today.
        8:*^C
   *Q
   Abort edit (Y/N)?_
```

When you enter Q, EDLIN asks if you really don't want to save the file. You then enter Y (for yes) if you really mean to use the Q command. If you enter N (or any other character), you'll see the EDLIN asterisk again and you can enter another command.

If you *do* want to save the new file, you use the E command to end the edit session. Here's how it looks:

```
        7:*DOS is with us today.
        8:*^C
   *E
   A>_
```

When EDLIN encounters the E command, the lines in memory are written to the $$$ file that was set up when EDLIN was initiated. The file is then renamed to use your extension and control returns to the DOS command processor. Now you can enter other DOS commands.

(a)   What two commands end the EDLIN program?_____

(b)   What EDLIN termination command causes the new or edited file to be saved

on disk?_____

_____

(c) What EDLIN termination command causes the new or edited file to be abandoned (not saved)?_____

(d) Which EDLIN termination command issues this message: Abort edit (Y/N)?

_____

(e) Suppose you see this message: Abort edit (Y/N)? What do you see if you type A and press Enter?

_____ A. *_

_____ B. A>_

_____ C. 8:*

_ _ _ _ _ _ _ _ _ _

(a) E and Q (b) E (c) Q (d) Q (e) A (anything other than Y cancels Q)

EDITING EXISTING FILES

8. When you provide the name of an existing file with EDLIN, you can edit that file. If you enter EDLIN FILE1.NEW after you created it and saved it with an E command, you'll see this:

```
End of input file
*_
```

This means the entire file has been read into memory. EDLIN always keeps a backup copy of the file you are editing. When you start editing FILE1.NEW, the new version is kept in FILE1.$$$; FILE1.NEW is not touched. When you finish the editing session and save the new version (using the E command), here's what happens:

```
FILE1.NEW becomes FILE1.BAK
FILE1.$$$ becomes FILE1.NEW
```

So the file named FILE1.NEW is the new version, and FILE1.BAK is the old version. The BAK file gives you an extra measure of safety.

When you start editing an existing file, EDLIN immediately erases any BAK file for that filename and opens up a $$$ file. So your backup file is gone as soon as you start the editing session. And for this reason, you can't edit a BAK file.

If you use a Q command to end an edit of an existing file, the $$$ version is erased and the former file remains unchanged.

Assume your file PRACTICE was created and edited earlier. There is also a PRACTICE.BAK file on the disk.

(a) What command do you use to edit the file?

A>_____

(b) Which files are on the disk after your command is issued?

_____ A. PRACTICE

_____ B. PRACTICE.BAK

_____ C. PRACTICE.$$$

(c) You want to terminate the edit session without saving any changes. What command do you use?_____

(d) Which files are on the disk now?

_____ A. PRACTICE

_____ B. PRACTICE.BAK

_____ C. PRACTICE.$$$

(e) Instead, suppose you want to terminate the edit session and save the changed version. What command do you use?_____

(f) Which files are on the disk now?

_____ A. PRACTICE

_____ B. PRACTICE.BAK

_____ C. PRACTICE.$$$

(g) *Extra thought question:* Suppose you now want to edit PRACTICE.BAK. How can you do that?

_____

_ _ _ _ _ _ _ _ _ _

(a) EDLIN PRACTICE (b) A, C; (c) Q (d) A (e) E (f) A, B; (g) RENAME it so it's not a BAK file

LISTING FILES

9. When you begin to edit an existing file, the console screen looks like this:

```
A>EDLIN FILE1.NEW
End of input file
*_
```

The entire file is in memory. You can see where the current line is by using the L command to list the data set on the console. In our example, you'd see this:

```
*L
        1:*This is the first line.
        2: This is the second line.
        3: This is the third line.
   *_
```

The current line is indicated with an asterisk. If you use the I command here, you'll see this next:

```
*I
        1:*
```

New lines can be inserted before the current line if you use I alone. Remember that Ctrl-Break ends insert mode.

You can insert new lines anywhere you wish if you specify a line number before I. If you use 1I, you can insert lines before the first line, for example. If you want to add lines to the end of the file, use a # sign. #I will let you add lines after the last line in the file. Each new line, wherever you add it, becomes the current line.

Suppose you want to add an extra line after line 2. Here's how you might do it:

```
*3I
        3:*This is an extra second line.
        4:*(Ctrl-Break)
*L
        1: This is the first line.
        2: This is the second line.
        3: This is an extra second line.
        4:*This is the third line.
   *_
```

Notice that the last line is renumbered and is now the current line.

(a) What command do you use to display a file being edited on the console?

_____

(b) What line is current when an existing file is first accessed under EDLIN?

_____

(c) What command would you use to add lines before the first line in a file?

_____

(d) What command would you use to add new lines between lines 6 and 7 in a file? _____

(e)   What command would you use to add lines to the end of an existing file?

_____

(f)   How do you end insert mode? _____

_ _ _ _ _ _ _ _ _ _

(a) L (b) the first line; (c) 1I (d) 7I (e) I (f) Ctrl-Break

10.   You've seen that the L command may list an entire file on the console. This is true only with short files. Actually, you can specify which lines should be listed. If you don't (as when you use L alone), the current line with 11 lines before and after it are listed. This is a full screen of data, since you get the EDLIN * prompt on the twenty-fourth line.

You can use one or two separate line numbers preceding L. If you use two, they must be separated by a comma or a space, as in 1,5L. You can use a space before L, also, if you like. If you use just the second line number, it must be preceded by a comma, as in ,5L. The first line number gives the first line number to be listed. If you omit it, the default first line is 11 lines before the current line. The second line number gives the last line to be listed. If you use the first line number and omit the second one, 23 lines are displayed starting with the specified line.

Suppose a file contains 50 lines (numbered 1 to 50, of course). If you use 1,23L, you'll see the first 23 lines, no matter which line is current. If the current line is one of those 23, it will be marked with an asterisk. If you use 1 L, you have omitted the second line number. Lines 1 through 23 will be listed. If you use ,23L you have omitted the first line number. Lines will be listed beginning 11 lines before the current line and ending with line 23.

Let's consider a file with 40 lines. The current line is 15.

(a)   What range of lines is listed for each of these commands?

_____   A.   L

_____   B.   6 L

_____   C.   ,20 L

_____   D.   2,8 L

_____   E.   30 40 L

(b)   What command will list lines 8, 9, 10, 11, and 12? _____

(c)   What command will list the first half of the file? _____

(d)   What command will list the last half of the file? _____

_ _ _ _ _ _ _ _ _ _

(a) A. 4–26; B. 6–29; C. 4–20; D. 2–8; E. 30–40; (b) 8,12 L or 8 12 L or 8 12L or 8,12L (not 812 L) (c) 1,20 L (d) 21,40 L

11.   There are a few exceptions in the use of the L command. For example, suppose you use L alone for a file with 15 lines. Line 2 is the current line. The display will show lines 1 through 15. Whenever there aren't 11 lines before the current line, extra lines after the current line will be listed, to the end of the file or to make a total of 23 lines.

Another exception occurs when you omit the first line number. Let's consider a file with 50 lines. Line 40 is current. You specify ,25 L. What is listed? The default first line is 11 lines before the current line, or 29. EDLIN can't list lines 29 through 25, and so it ignores your 25 and displays 23 lines centered around line 40. If you specified ,30 L instead, lines 29 and 30 would be listed. If the specified line is more than 11 lines before the current line, the list is the same as if you omitted both line numbers.

You may on occasion list more lines than will fit on the console screen. In that case, use Ctrl-NumLock to pause the display. Any character except Ctrl-Break will restart it; Ctrl-Break cancels the command.

If the first line number you enter is larger than the second, as in 25,2L, you'll get the message "Entry error." You can correct the command and reenter it. If you happen to use the wrong format and put L first in a command, EDLIN will interpret it as just L and give you the default screenful. Thus L1,20 will produce a listing centered around the current line.

Now consider a file that contains 60 lines. Line 5 is current.

(a)   What range of lines is listed for each of these commands?

_____ A.   10 L

_____ B.   L

_____ C.   ,30 L

_____ D.   ,10 L

(b)   What range of lines is listed for each of these commands if line 30 is current?

_____ A.   10 L

_____ B.   L

_____ C.   ,10 L

_____ D.   ,30 L

(c)   Write a command to list five lines before and after current line 30. _____

(d)   Write a command to list the entire file. _____

(e)   How can you pause the listing of the entire file? _____

(f)   How can you restart the listing of the entire file? _____

(g)   How can you cancel the listing of the entire file? _____

(a) A. 10–32; B. 1–23; C. 1–23; D. 1–10; (b) A. 10–32; B. 19–41; C. 19–41; D. 19–30; (c) 25,35 L (d) 1,60 L (e) Ctrl-NumLock; (f) any character; (g) Ctrl-Break

In this chapter, you've seen how to create a file, insert lines into it, list it, and store it or abandon it. There isn't much that can go wrong. If you enter EDLIN without naming a file, you'll get the message "Filename must be specified." If you use line number incorrectly with the L command, you'll get a different result than you expect.

In the next chapter, we'll focus on editing within any specific line in an EDLIN file.

Chapter Eight Self-Test

1. Suppose you want to create a new file named COMMANDS.ED.

   Write the command you would use. _____

2. The console screen shows this:

   ```
   New file
   *_
   ```

   You want to add lines to the file. What command do you use first?

   *_____

3. The console screen shows this line:

   ```
   1:*_
   ```

   What do you do to enter the line "EDLIN Commands"?_____

4. The console screen shows this:

   ```
   1:*EDLIN Commands
   2:*_
   ```

   How can you stop adding lines?

   _____

5. The console screen looks like this:

```
*I
      1:*EDLIN Commands
     ·2:*
*_
```

What command would you enter if you want to abandon the file and not save it on disk?

_____

6. The console screen looks like this:

```
*I
        1:*EDLIN Commands
        2:*
*_
```

What command should you enter if you want to save the file by storing it on disk?

_____

7. Now suppose you want to edit the file and add more lines. You enter the EDLIN command again and see this:

```
End of input file
*_
```

What do you enter to display the contents of the file?

`*`_____

8. The console screen shows this:

```
        1:*EDLIN Commands
     *
```

What do you enter to begin adding lines at the end of the file?

`*`_____

Suppose you are editing a file that contains 30 lines. Line 25 is current.

9. What command will list the first 15 lines on the console?

A>_____

10. What command will list the last 15 lines on the console?

    A>_____

11. What lines will be listed by L? _____

12. What lines will be listed by 2L? _____

Self-Test Answer Key

1. EDLIN COMMANDS.ED
2. I
3. Type the line and press Enter
4. Press Ctrl-Break or Ctrl-Z
5. Q
6. E
7. L
8. #I
9. 1,15L
10. 16,30L
11. Lines 14 through 30
12. Lines 2 through 24

Suggested Machine Exercise

1. Boot the computer with your backup system disk. Check the directory to make sure EDLIN.COM is on the disk. Insert a formatted disk in drive B. This disk can contain other data, but it should have at least 20K of available space.

2. Create a new file called B:ED1.ME. Enter these six lines into the file:

   ```
   1   EDITED FILE
   2   This is the first file I have edited.
   3   In the process, I've used several different
   4   editing commands.
   5   When I was finished, I stored
   6   the file on disk.
   ```

   Use backspace as needed, but don't worry about your typing.

3. Save the file on disk.

4. Call up the file again under EDLIN and list it on the console.

5. Insert one line at the beginning; put your name on that line.

6. List the first three lines on your printer.

7. Abandon the edited file, but save your original, as you'll edit it after completing the next chapter.

CHAPTER NINE
Using Editing Keys Under EDLIN

The EDLIN program operates on lines. You will often need to modify data in individual lines in your file. You do this using the DOS editing keys after selecting a line under EDLIN.

When you are first entering a line, you can make corrections with backspace and overtyping before you press Enter. The content of the line when you press Enter is placed in memory. Most times, however, you will make corrections later. In this chapter, you'll see how you can change lines after they have been entered.

When you have finished this chapter, you will be able to:

- Select a line for editing
- Use the Ins and Del keys to add or remove characters in a line
- Use the F1 key to copy one character to the monitor
- Use the F2 key to copy all characters up to a specified one to the monitor
- Use the F3 key to copy all characters to the monitor
- Use the F4 key to skip over all characters, up to a specified one
- Use the F5 key to continue editing a partially edited line

THE EDIT LINE COMMAND

1. In EDLIN you can edit a specific line if you enter the line number at the EDLIN * prompt. Here's the result:

```
*2
        2: This is the second line.
        2:*_
```

EDLIN shows you the line and makes it current. Now you can type in a complete new line if you wish. When you press Enter after typing changes, the new line is stored in the file and remains current.

If you want to edit the current line, or just find out what it is, you can just type a period (.) at the * prompt. If you want to move down a line—that is, make the next line current, display it, and possibly edit it—just press Enter in response to the * prompt.

If you press Enter at the very beginning of the line, you'll see the EDLIN * prompt again. This cancels your edit line request and keeps the line as it was before. If you type even one space or character before pressing enter, then Enter ends the new line and eliminates the old one.

If you change your mind about editing a line after you've gotten started, you can cancel it with Esc or Ctrl-Break. This will leave the original line unchanged and restore the EDLIN * prompt. The line you were editing remains current.

Suppose your console shows this:

```
*L
     1:*Microcomputers are a great invention.
     2: They provide hours of fun and work
     3: to children and adults every day.
*_
```

(a) What would you enter to change line 2? _____

This appears on the console:

```
     2: They provide hours of fun and work
     2:*_
```

(b) What happens if you press Enter now?

_____ A. Line 2 is eliminated

_____ B. Line 2 is unchanged

(c) What does line 2 contain if you type "I think" then press Enter?

_____ A. I think

_____ B. I think They provide hours of fun and work

_____ C. I thinkovide hours of fun and work

_____ D. Nothing; it is eliminated

(d) Suppose instead you type "I think" and then press Ctrl-Break. What does line 2 contain now?

_____ A. I think

_____ B. They provide hours of fun and work

_____ C. Nothing; it is eliminated

(e)   Suppose the console looks like this:

```
    *2
            2:  They provide hours of fun and work
            2:*I think they are useful (Esc)
        *
```

What does line 2 contain?

_____ A.   They provide hours of fun and work

_____ B.   I think they are useful

_____ C.   Nothing; it has been eliminated

(f)   What would you enter at the asterisk to let you edit the current line? ___

_ _ _ _ _ _ _ _ _ _

(a) 2; (b) B; (c) A; (d) B; (e) A; (f) period (.)

The edit line command allows you to edit any line by replacing it with whatever you type. You can use the DOS editing keys along with Ins and Del to simplify making changes to existing lines. These keys are labeled F1 through F5 and are located on the left side of your keyboard.

Before we talk about the effects of each key, however, you should understand how EDLIN handles your data lines.

THE INPUT BUFFER

2.   Whatever line is current is stored in a special memory area called an *input buffer*. If you are typing in a new line, a copy is being created in two places. One is on the console screen where you see it. When you backspace and overtype, the copy on the screen changes. Another copy is created inside the computer in the input buffer. This is kept exactly like what you see on the screen, but it is done internally. When you are satisfied with a line as it appears on the screen, you press Enter. The line is actually written to the file from the input buffer. When you are entering a new line, backspacing and retyping is the only form of editing you can do. Once a line is entered, however, you can call it up for changes. Then you can use other methods of changing the line.

The Insert (Ins) and Delete (Del) keys on your keyboard affect the input buffer as well as the screen. When you are changing a line but have not yet pressed Enter, the cursor on the screen matches a character pointer in the input buffer. If you press Del, the character at the cursor on the screen and the corresponding character in the input buffer are deleted. The cursor stays where it is. If you press Del repeatedly (or hold it down so it repeats), you can take out a whole string of characters. If you press Ins, the next character you type will appear at the cursor.

Whatever was at the cursor location will be pushed to the right. You can insert many characters in this way. Until you press Enter or press another DOS editing key, any characters you type will be inserted. Just as with Del, Ins changes the input buffer as it changes the screen display.

Suppose you are entering a new line. It looks like this on the screen:

        8:*The buffer is is 253 characters_

(a) You notice that the word "is" appears twice. How can you correct it?

    _____ A. Backspace to the beginning of the second "is" and retype the second half of the line

    _____ B. Backspace to the beginning of one "is" and press Del three times

(b) Now the line looks like this:

        8:*The buffer is 253 characters

You decide that you should have written "input buffer." How can you correct this?

    _____ A. Backspace to the beginning of "buffer" and retype "input buffer is 253 characters"

    _____ B. Backspace to the beginning of "buffer", press Ins, and type "input"

(c) Now the line looks like this:

        8:*The input buffer is 253 characters_

You want to add the word "long" and a period to the end of the line and send the line to the file. How do you do this?

    _____ A. Type " long." and press Enter.

    _____ B. Press Ins, type " long." and press Enter.

    _____ C. Type " long." and press Ctrl-Break.

(d) When you press Enter, what is stored in the input buffer?

    _____

(e) Which of the following indicates when you can use the Ins and Del keys to correct a line?

    _____ A. Whenever you are entering a new line under EDLIN

    _____ B. Whenever you are in insert mode under EDLIN

    _____ C. When you are editing a line that was entered earlier under EDLIN

_ _ _ _ _ _ _ _ _ _

(a) A; (b) A; (c) A or B (pressing Ins won't have any effect, but it won't do any harm either); (d) The input buffer is 253 characters long.; (e) C

F1 AND F3

3.   Now let's talk about how you use the DOS editing keys when you edit a line. You've already seen how you can edit a specific line by entering its line number when you see the EDLIN asterisk prompt. We'll consider F1 and F3 first.

Every time you press F1, one character from the buffer is copied to the screen. The cursor moves along with it. Here's an example:

```
    *6

         6:*The input buffer serves as a template.
         6:*_
```

If you press F1 four times, the screen looks like this:

```
    *6

         6:*The input buffer serves as a template.
         6:*The_
```

Now you could press Ins and type "DOS". Then press F1 three more times. Now the screen looks like this:

```
    *6

         6:*The input buffer serves as a template.
         6:*The DOS in_
```

You can continue to use F1 to copy each character from the buffer, or you can use F3. F3 copies the rest of the line from the buffer to the screen. If you press F3 for the example above, the screen will look like this:

```
    *6

         6: The input buffer serves as a template.
         6:*The DOS input buffer serves as a template._
```

You can now press Enter and the new line is stored. Or you can add more characters to the end of the line. EDLIN is automatically in insert mode when the cursor is at the end of a line.

(a) Name the DOS editing key that performs each of these functions:

_____ A. Remove the character at the cursor

_____ B. Put in a new character at the cursor, pushing other characters to the right

_____ C. Copy one character from the buffer to the screen, moving the cursor

_____ D. Copy the rest of the characters from the buffer to the screen

(b) Suppose the screen looks like this:

```
12:*The insert key lets you add characters.
12:*_
```

You want to change "insert" to Ins. Complete the steps below:

A. Use the _____ key _____ times to position cursor at "i".

B. Use the _____ key _____ times to remove the word "insert".

C. Use the _____ key to allow you to add the new word.

D. Type _____ .

E. Use the _____ key to copy the rest of the buffer to the screen.

_ _ _ _ _ _ _ _ _ _

(a) A. Del, B. Ins, C. F1, D. F3; (b) A. F1, 4; B. Del, 6; C. Ins; D. Ins; E. F3

4. Let's see another way you can use the buffer before looking at other DOS editing keys. Suppose the screen looks like this:

```
*6
        6:*The insert key lets you add characters.
        6:*_
```

When you type, you replace characters in the buffer, just as you do on the screen. For example, you could change "insert" to "Ins" without using the Ins key. Use these steps:

- F1 four times   (6:*The_)
- Type "Ins"   (6:*The Ins_)
- Del three times   (6:*The Ins_)
- F3   (6:*The Ins key lets you add characters._)

Notice that the characters typed in (Ins) overlaid the characters that formerly occupied those positions.

Suppose the screen looks like this:

```
*7
        7:*The Fl key copies one character.
        7:*_
```

You want to modify the line so it reads "F1 copies one character. It is useful." You could, of course, retype the entire line. Once you get used to the DOS editing keys, however, you'll find they save a great deal of time. In this frame, we'll use the editing keys.

(a) The first step is to change the line so it begins "F1".

What key do you press first?_____

How many times?_____

(b) Now the screen looks like this:

```
*7
        7:*The Fl key copies one character.
        7:*_
```

You have eliminated "The " from the buffer. The next step is to eliminate "key ".

What key do you press next?_____

How many times?_____

(c) Now the screen looks like this:

```
*7
        7:*The Fl key copies one character.
        7:*Fl_
```

What key do you press next?_____

How many times?_____

(d) The next step is to add information ("It is useful.") to the end of the original line. What key copies the rest of the original line?_____

(e) How do you add the information?_____

(f) How could you cancel the changed line and restore the original one? ___
_____

(g) How could you store the changed line after (e) above? _____

―――――――――――

(a) Del, 4; (b) F1, 3; (c) Del, 4; (d) F3; (e) just type it (Ins is automatic at end of line); (f) Esc or Ctrl-Break; (g) press Enter

LEFT AND RIGHT ARROWS

5.   The left and right arrows on the numeric keypad can also be used during editing. The right arrow has the same effect as F1; it copies a single character from the buffer and moves the character pointer one position. The left arrow has the opposite effect; it erases one character from the screen and moves the character pointer back one position in the buffer. This can be very useful if you copied too many characters from the buffer. Suppose the console contains this:

```
4:*The left arrrrow moves the pointer backwards.
4:*The left arrrrow_
```

You had intended to remove a few of the "r" characters. Just press the left arrow on the numeric keypad four times. Now the console will contain this:

```
4:*The left arrrrow moves the pointer backwards.
4:*The left arr_
```

Now you can press Del two times, press F3 to copy the rest of the line, and the correction is made.

(a)   Which two keys can be used to copy a single character from the buffer?

_____ A.   F1

_____ B.   F3

_____ C.   Right arrow on numeric keypad

_____ D.   Left arrow on numeric keypad

(b)   Which key can be used to move the character pointer in the buffer backwards one character? _____

―――――――――――

(a) A, C; (b) left arrow on numeric keypad

THE F2 KEY

6. Now you know how to use F1 to copy a single character from the buffer to the screen, and F3 to copy whatever remains. Another DOS editing key, F2, can be used to copy characters up to a certain point.

Suppose the screen looks like this:

```
2:*The right arrow has the same effect as F1.
2:*_
```

Notice that "arrow" has an extra "r" in it. You could use F1 eleven times to get over there and delete one "r". The F2 key offers a shortcut. If you press F2 and then enter "a", all letters from the buffer up to the first "a" are copied to the screen, which now looks like this:

```
2:*The right arrow has the same effect as F1.
2:*The right_
```

Now you can press F1 to copy the "a", press Del to remove one "r", and press F3 to copy the rest of the line.

You may wonder why we didn't press F2 and type "r". If we had done that, the screen would have looked like this:

```
2:*The right arrow has the same effect as F1.
2:*The_
```

The first "r" was not what we wanted. We would have to press F2 again, and type "r" again. It was a bit quicker the first way.

Keep in mind that F2 is just a shortcut; it saves you using lots of F1s. But you never *have* to use F2. Let's try using F2 in a paper example now.

The screen looks like this:

```
9:*Press F2; type one character.
9:*
```

You want to change line 9 to read "Press F2, then type one character."

(a) How do you skip over to the semicolon?

_____ A. Press F1 eight times

_____ B. Press F2, then type ";"

_____ C. Press F3

(b)   The screen now looks like this:

```
9:*Press F2; type one character.
9:*Press F2_
```

How can you change the semicolon to a comma?_____

(c)   How do you copy the next space to the screen?_____

(d)   How can you add the word "then"?_____

(e)   How can you copy the rest of the buffer to the screen?_____

(f)   How do you store the edited line in the file?_____

— — — — — — — — —

(a) A or B; (b) just type ","; (c) press F1; (d) use Ins, type "then "; (e) press F3; (f) press Enter

THE F4 KEY

7.   You've seen that F2 can be used to have the effect of several consecutive uses of F1. Another DOS editing key can be used to have the effect of several consecutive uses of Del. When you press F4, followed by typing a single character, all characters in the buffer from the character pointer up to the next occurrence of that character are deleted. Suppose the screen looks like this:

```
2:*The right arrow has the same effect as F1.
2:*
```

Suppose you want to change the line to read "The right arrow or F1 copies one character." You first press F2 and type "w". The lines look like this:

```
2:*The right arrow has the same effect as F1.
2:*The right arro_
```

Now press F1 (or the right arrow) twice. The cursor is positioned after the space. Type "or". Now press F4 and type "F". Press F1 twice. Now the screen looks like this:

```
2:*The right arrow has the same effect as F1.
2:*The right arrow or F1_
```

Now you simply type the rest of the new line.

F4 is the opposite of F2, in a sense. Where F2 copies all characters up to the specified one, F4 deletes them all. F2 is a way of conserving F1 keystrokes. F4 is a way of conserving Del keystrokes.

Suppose the screen looks like this:

```
3:*The DOS editing keys let you edit within a line.
3:*
```

You want to change the line to "DOS editing keys are used for within a line editing."

(a)   How would you delete "The " from the beginning of the line?

_____ A.   Press Del four times

_____ B.   Press F4; then type "D"

_____ C.   Type four blanks

(b)   How would you copy "DOS editing keys " to the screen?

_____ A.   Press Fl, 17 times

_____ B.   Press F2; then type "1"

_____ C.   Press F3; the backspace

(c)   Now the screen looks like this:

```
3:*The DOS editing keys let you edit within a line.
3:*DOS editing keys_
```

How can you eliminate "let you edit "?

_____ A.   Press Del 13 times

_____ B.   Press F4; then type "w"

_____ C.   Press F2; then type "w"

(d)   How can you add "are used for" before "within"?_____

(e)   How can you copy "within a line" to the screen?_____

(f)   Now the screen looks like this:

```
3:*The DOS editing keys let you edit within a line
3:*DOS editing keys are used for within a line_
```

How do you add "editing." and save the line?_____

—————————

(a) A or B; (b) A or B; (c) A or B; (d) press Ins, and then type "are used for"; (e) press F2, and then type "." or use F1 repeatedly; (f) just type "editing." and press Enter

THE F5 KEY

8.   You have seen how to use the Ins and Del keys, as well as the F1, F2, F3, and F4. You may have noticed that it is possible to get confused about what is in the buffer, especially if you've used Del and F4 very much. The F5 key gives you a new line to work with and puts the currently edited line in the buffer for further editing. The line isn't changed in the file; you can still cancel it with Esc or Ctrl-Break.

   F5 moves the line as currently displayed into the buffer. The effect is similar to pressing Enter, but the line isn't saved yet. Here's an example:

```
        3:*The DOS editing keys let you edit within a line.
        3:*DOS editing keys are used for within a line editing.@
          _
```

The @ character is displayed when you press F5. It shows which line is the current buffer. If you press Enter immediately, the line is saved. If you press F3, you'll see how the buffer looks.

   As shown above, you can continue to edit the line using overtyping and any or all of the DOS editing keys.

(a)   Name the DOS editing key that accomplishes each function below.

   _____ A. Copy all characters up to a specified character

   _____ B. Delete all characters up to a specified character

   _____ C. Copy one character

   _____ D. Delete one character

   _____ E. Copy the rest of the characters

   _____ F. Replace the buffer with the currently displayed line

(b)   Suppose a screen looks like this:

```
        4:*The DOS editing key Fl copies one character.
        4:*DOS editing key Fl can be used to @
          _
```

   Now you press F2 and type "F". What will the last screen line contain?

_____

(c) Look at the screen display in question (b). What DOS editing key was pressed at @? _____

— — — — — — — — — —

(a) A—F2; B—F4; C—F1; D—Del; E—F3; F—F5; (b) "DOS editing key "; (c) F5

9. What DOS editing key has each effect below?

_____ (a) Copy the rest of the characters from the buffer

_____ (b) Insert one character into the buffer

_____ (c) Delete one character from the buffer

_____ (d) Copy one character from the buffer

_____ (e) Delete all characters from the buffer up to the next occurrence of a specified character

_____ (f) Copy all characters from the buffer up to the next occurrence of a specified character

_____ (g) Replace the buffer with the current edited line, but don't store it in the file

_____ (h) Store the current edited line

— — — — — — — — — —

(a) F3; (b) Ins; (c) Del; (d) F1; (e) F4; (f) F2; (g) F5; (h) Enter

In this chapter, you have learned to use the DOS editing keys. You should now be able to create and edit a file on your DOS system.

Chapter Nine Self-Test

1. Suppose you are editing a file. You want to find out what line is current.

   a. What do you type at the prompt? * _____

   b. What do you do to cancel the edit request and leave that line current?

   _____

2. Suppose you are editing a file. What do you enter to begin changing line 1?

   * _____

3. The console screen now looks like this:

```
1: EDLIN Commands
1:*_
```

Suppose you want to change the line to "Summary of EDLIN commands." Which of the following is the quickest way to accomplish the change?

_____ (a) Retype the line, making the changes.

_____ (b) Use F1 to copy the current part; then make the changes.

_____ (c) Press Ins, and then type "Summary of"; then press F2.

_____ (d) Press Ins, and then type "Summary of"; then press F3.

_____ (e) Type "Summary of"; then press F3.

4. What key do you press to accomplish each of the following?

a. Delete the character at the cursor. _____

b. Delete all characters from the one at the cursor to the next occurence of a specified character. _____

c. End the line and store it. _____

d. Cancel the line edit and restore the original line. _____

5. What key do you press to accomplish each of the following?

a. Copy one character from the buffer to the screen. _____

b. Copy the rest of the characters in the buffer to the screen. _____

c. Copy all characters from the current location of the character pointer until the next occurrence of a specified character. _____

d. Add a character at the character pointer. _____

6. Which DOS editing key can you use to replace the line currently being edited in the buffer without storing it in the file?_____

Suppose you are editing a file that contains 30 lines. Line 25 is current.

7. What command will list the first 15 lines on the console? A>_____

8. What command will list the last 15 lines on the console? A>_____

9. What lines will be listed by L?_____

10. What lines will be listed by 2L?_____

Self-Test Answer Key

1. a. Period (.)
   b. Press Enter immediately, or Ctrl-Break
2. *1
3. d
4. (a) Del
   (b) F4
   (c) Enter
   (d) Ctrl-Break or Esc
5. (a) F1
   (b) F3
   (c) F2
   (d) Ins
6. F5
7. 1,15L
8. 16,30L
9. Lines 14 through 30
10. Lines 2 through 24

Suggested Machine Excercise

In this exercise, you will edit the file you created in the last chapter. If you didn't save it, re-enter this data as B:ED1.ME and save the file.

```
1   EDITED FILE
2   This is the first file I have edited.
3   In the process, I've used several different
4   editing commands.
5   When I was finished, I stored
6   the file on disk.
```

1. Now call up the file for some changes.
   a. Change line 2 to read "This is the very first file I have edited.".
   b. Change line 4 to read "editing commands, including I and E.".
   c. Change line 5 to read "When I finished, I stored".
   d. Change line 6 to read "the edited file on a disk.", and then cancel your change.
   e. Change line 6 to read "the entire file on disk", and then put the change in the buffer. Then, add a period and store the line.
   f. Add a new line 7 "The DOS editing keys are useful.".
   g. Add a blank line before and after the original line 2.

2. List the entire file on the console.

3. List the first three lines on the console and on the printer.

4. Add about 20 lines, using just one word per line, such as "one", "two", "three", etc.

5. Set line 10 as current.

6. List the first 10 lines on the console.

7. Save the entire file; you'll edit it some more at the end of the next chapter.

8. Now call up the file again and experiment with it. Use all the DOS editing keys. Change lines, list lines, generally get familiar with EDLIN commands. When you are finished experimenting, abandon your changes.

CHAPTER TEN

The DOS Editing Functions

You know the basics of using EDLIN now to prepare files on your Personal Computer. In this chapter, you'll learn some more features of EDLIN that will make modifying and preparing files easier and more effective.

Up to now, we've been considering fairly small files that fit completely into memory. In this chapter, you'll learn to handle larger files with new EDLIN commands and techniques.

When you complete your study of this chapter, you will be able to:

- Use lines longer than the screen width
- Delete or duplicate a line in the file
- Search the file for a specific string of characters
- Replace a specific string of characters with another, wherever it occurs
- Create and edit files that are too large to fit in memory

LINES LONGER THAN 80 CHARACTERS

1. Each line in an EDLIN file can be up to 253 characters long. This is wider than the console screen. When you are in insert mode, you have 72 positions remaining on the screen line, since leading spaces and the line number take up eight positions.

If you enter a line longer than 72 characters, it will automatically wrap around to continue in column 1 of the next line. You could have a single-numbered line that occupies three full console lines and part of a fourth line, with 72 characters on the first line, 80 characters on each of the next two lines, and 21 characters on the fourth line, for a total of 253 characters. Then, you should press Enter. If you continue typing, the 254th character will be quietly accepted. On the next character, the console will beep and no more will be accepted. If you press Enter now, the line will contain 254 characters. This line will be safely stored and saved as part of the file, but you won't be able to edit it. If you need to make any changes to a 254-character line, you'll need to retype the entire line.

Another problem may arise if lines are longer than the console width. Suppose you have a series of 100-character lines as lines 6 through 12. Each will use two console lines. If you want a printout of the lines, you press Ctrl-PrtSc and then use the command 6,12L. The lines display nicely on the console. On the printer, however, only one line is used for each file line. If you are printing 80 characters per line rather than 132 characters per line, the second print line (28 characters) will *overprint* the first print line. You will find that the first part of each line is double printed and unreadable. The printer advances to a new line when it encounters a carriage return. You can handle this problem for lines up to 132 characters long by using a MODE command before entering EDLIN. Another option is to use Shift-PrtScr (the screen print function). This will print a copy of the screen no matter how the lines are arranged.

(a) What is the maximum length for an editable line in an EDLIN file? _____

(b) What is the longest line EDLIN will let you enter? _____

(c) What happens if you use echo printing to list a line that contains 150 characters?

_____ A. It prints just as it appears on the console.

_____ B. The lines overprint on the console and on the printer.

_____ C. The line will occupy two lines on the console, but will overprint on the printer.

(d) What command can you use while in EDLIN to allow you to print a readable copy of a 132-character line?

_____ A. TYPE 132

_____ B. MODE 132

_____ C. MODE LPT1: 132

_____ D. Shift-PrtScr

_____ E. Ctrl-PrtScr

(e) What command can you use before entering EDLIN that will allow you to print 132 characters on one printer line while in EDLIN?

_____ A. TYPE 132

_____ B. MODE 132

_____ C. MODE LPT1: 132

_____ D. Shift-PrtScr

_____ E. Ctrl-PrtScr

- - - - - - - - -

(a) 253 characters; (b) 254 characters; (c) C; (d) D; (e) C

DUPLICATING LINES

2. You learned in the last chapter to use the DOS editing keys while modifying lines. There are a few more things you can do with those keys. One of the most useful techniques is to duplicate a line.

Suppose a short file contains these lines:

```
*i
    1:*                    LISTING OF TASKS
    2:*Task                   Person                     Priority
    3:*                    David Smith                       1
    3:*End of task list
    5:*^C
```

You want to enter several more lines just like the current line 3. The first step is to get the contents of line 3 into the input buffer. Then you can enter insert mode again and use F3 to copy the line as many times as needed. Here's how such an interaction might look:

```
                    *3
                        3:*        David Smith      1
    (use F3)            3:*        David Smith      1      (Enter)
                    *4i
    (use F3)            4:*        David Smith      1      (Enter)
    (use F3)            5:*        David Smith      1      (Enter)
    (use F3)            6:*        David Smith      1      (Enter)
    (use Ctrl-Break)    7:^C
                    *L
                        1:*            LISTING OF TASKS
                        2:*Task          Person        Priority
                        3:*        David Smith       1
                        4:*        David Smith       1
                        5:*        David Smith       1
                        6:*        David Smith       1
                        7:*End of task list
                    *
```

You can now edit the lines to insert specific tasks. Here's an example:

```
*3
    3:*                        David Smith    1
    3:*Survey workers<F3>      David Smith    1
*4
    4:*                        David Smith    1
    4:*Analyze results<F3>     David Smith    1
*5
    5:*                        David Smith    1
    5:*Send thank yous<F3>     David Smith    1
*6
    6:*                        David Smith    1
    6:*Write report<F3>        David Smith    1
*5
    5:*Send thank yous         David Smith    1
    5:*<F2-1>Send thank yous   David Smith    _(type 2;
                                               press Enter)
*L
    1:          LISTING OF TASKS
    2:  Task                Person      Priority
    3:  Survey workers      David Smith    1
    4:  Analyze results     David Smith    1
    5:*Send thank yous      David Smith    2
    6:  Write report        David Smith    1
    7:  End of task list
```

By using the input buffer, we saved time and effort in creating the file. Suppose you have this file:

```
    1:  Pencils
    2:  Paper, narrow ruled
    3:  Pens
    4:  File folders
```

You want to include three more types of paper. You can do this by repeating line 2 three more times. You decide to put the new lines at the end of the file.

(a) What command will put the line to be duplicated in the input buffer?

*_____

(b) The console looks like this:

```
        2:*Paper, narrow ruled
        2:*_
```

You press F3, then Enter. Now the console looks like this:

```
        2:*Paper, narrow ruled
        2:*Paper, narrow ruled
   *_
```

What command will let you insert new lines at the end of the file?

*_____

(c) The console looks like this:

```
   5:*_
```

What will copy the contents of the input buffer to this new line?

_____

(d) The console looks like this:

```
   5:*Paper, narrow ruled_
```

You want to add "legal sized" to this line. How can you do this?

_____ A. You must press Ins and then type "legal sized".

_____ B. Just type "legal sized".

_____ C. End insert mode; then edit the line.

(e) The console looks like this:

```
   5:*Paper, narrow ruled legal sized
   6:*_
```

You want the next line to read "Paper, wide ruled." How can you copy the first part of the input buffer to the new line?

_____ A. Press F2, then ","

_____ B. Press F2, then "n"

_____ C. Press F4, then ","

_____ D. Press F4, then "n"

(f)   The console looks like this;

```
5:*Paper, narrow ruled legal sized
6:*Paper, _
```

You type "wide" and press Del twice. What will copy the rest of the buffer to the line?

_____

(g)   What does the input buffer contain now?

_____

— — — — — — — — — —

(a) 2 (b) #i (c) F3 (d) B (e) B (f) F3 (g) Paper, wide ruled legal sized

3.   You have seen how you can copy the line in the input buffer to other places in the file. Whenever you modify the line, however, the modified line replaces the old one in the buffer.

Suppose you want to enter about 100 lines that all begin the same. The ending of each line is different, with varying lengths. If you enter each full line separately, this will take quite a while, depending on your typing speed. You can use the input buffer to speed it up. One approach is as follows;

```
A>EDLIN NEW100
New file
*I
          1:*This is a new line, the first. <Enter>
          2:*<F2-,>This is a new line. Number two. <Enter>
          3:*<F3>This is a new line. Number two. <use left
             arrow 3 times then type> hree. <Enter>
          4:*^C
  *_
```

We stopped here, but you get the idea. At the stopping point, the input buffer contains "This is a new line. Number three.". You can use any of the editing keys to take advantage of the input buffer as the source of a new line.

Another approach is to enter the constant part (this is a new line) first, then edit each line to complete it. Let's walk through that process, from the beginning. The console looks like this:

```
A>EDLIN APPROACH.2
New file
*_
```

(a) What command do you enter to begin? *_____

(b) The console looks like this:

```
1:*_
```

What do you enter for the constant part of the first line?

1:*_____

(c) The console looks like this:

```
1:*This is a new line
2:*_
```

How do you duplicate line 1? _____

(d) The console looks like this:

```
1:*This is a new line
2:*This is a new line_
```

How do you prepare for the next line? _____

(e) The console looks like this:

```
1:*This is a new line
2:*This is a new line
3:*_
```

How do you duplicate the line again? _____

(f) Assume you have done the same steps many times. The last few console lines look like this:

```
 98:*This is a new line
 99:*This is a new line
100:*This is a new line
101:*_
```

How do you stop duplicating the line and terminate insert mode? _____

(g) What command do you use to go back and edit the first line?*_____

— — — — — — — — — —

(a) i (b) "This is a new line" (c) F3 (d) press Enter; (e) F3 (f) Ctrl-Break (g) 1

DELETING LINES

4.   Duplicating lines with F3 is so easy, you may absentmindedly enter too many of them. EDLIN provides a delete command (D) to let you delete lines. You can use D alone to delete the current line, or precede it with one or two line numbers to delete a range of lines. For example, 5,10 D will cause lines 5 through 10 in the file to be deleted. The former line 11 becomes current and all following lines are automatically renumbered. Whenever you delete lines, no matter how many or where they are in relation to the current line, the line following the last deleted line becomes current.

Let's look at some examples. Suppose a file contains these lines:

```
1: LineA
2: LineB
3: LineC
4:*LineD
5: LineE
6: LineF
7: LineG
```

The command "d" will delete line 4, and renumber lines 5, 6, and 7. The new line 4 (LineE) will then be current. The command "2,4d" will delete lines 2, 3, and 4. The lines will be renumbered, and the original line 6 (LineF) will be current, as line 2. We deleted one line with D, then three with 2,4D. Here is the file after those two commands:

```
1: LineA
2:*LineF
3: LineG
```

Suppose you have a file that contains these lines:

```
 1: One partridge in a pear tree
 2: Two turtle doves
 3: Three French hens
 4: Four calling birds
 5: Five golden rings
 6:*Six geese a-laying
 7: Seven swans a-swimming
 8: Eight maids a-milking
 9: Nine ladies dancing
10: Ten lords a-leaping
*
```

(a)   What command will delete the current line?

    *_____

(b)   What line is current now?

    _____ A.   Five golden rings

    _____ B.   Six geese a-laying

    _____ C.   Seven swans a-swimming

    _____ D.   Eight maids a-milking

(c)   What command will delete the first four lines in the file?

    *_____

(d)   What line is current now?

    _____ A.   Four calling birds

    _____ B.   Five golden rings

    _____ C.   Six geese a-laying

    _____ D.   Seven swans a-swimming

(e)   How many lines are in the file now? _____

(f)   What line is numbered 3 after the deletions in (a) and (c)?

    _____ A.   Three French hens

    _____ B.   Five golden rings

    _____ C.   Seven swans a-swimming

    _____ D.   Eight maids a-milking

    _____ E.   Nine ladies dancing

- - - - - - - - - -

(a) d (b) c (c) 1,4d (d) B (e) 5 (f) D

5.   If you omit both line numbers before the delete command, the current line is deleted. If you include both line numbers, both those lines are deleted along with any lines between them. This will only work, of course, if the first line number is smaller than the second. If you enter something like "4,2D" you'll get the message "Entry error" with no lines deleted. Then you can correct your command and try again. If, however, you code "D2,4" or "D4,2" or anything with "D" first, the current line will be deleted with no error message. When EDLIN encounters "D" or "d" in the command area, it assumes the end of a delete command. You can get away with typing "delete" or "2,4delete" just as well, but it is quicker to just use "d."

You can use just one of the line numbers. If you use only the first, as in "4d" or "4,d", only that line will be deleted. The line following it will become current. If you want to delete line 205, simple enter "205d" at the EDLIN asterisk prompt. If you enter "d205", you'll delete the current line instead.

If you use only the second line number, by coding a comma before the number, deletion starts with the current line and continues through the line you specify. If line 8 is current, and you enter ",12d", lines 8 through 12 will be deleted. There is no short way to delete from a specified line number to the current line. You would have to use two line numbers.

Suppose you have this file:

```
 1:  One partridge in a pear tree
 2:  Two turtle doves
 3:  Three French hens
 4:  Four calling birds
 5:  Five golden rings
 6:*Six geese a-laying
 7:  Seven swans a-swimming
 8:  Eight maids a-milking
 9:  Nine ladies dancing
10:  Ten lords a-leaping
```

(a) Assume each of these commands is issued to the original file as shown. What line or lines will be deleted by each?

A. D_____

B. D1_____

C. 1D_____

D. 2,6DELETE_____

E. ,4D_____

F. 8,6D_____

(b) Assume the file is intact, as shown above. Write a command that will eliminate the line with "French hens."

_____

(c) What line is current after eliminating that line?

_____

(d) Write a command that will eliminate the first three lines from the file.

_____

(e) Assume the file is intact again. Write a command that will delete the first six lines. Remember that line 6 is current. _____

(f)   Assume the file is intact again. Write a command that will delete the last four lines. Remember that line 6 is current. _____

— — — — — — — — — —

(a) a—6, B—6, C—1, D—2, 3, 4, 5, 6, E—1, 2, 3, 4, F—none (entry error); (b) 3D (c) Four calling birds (now line 3); (d) 1,3D (e) 1,6D (1D or 1,D deletes only line 1); (f) 7,10D or ,10D

SEARCHING THE FILE

6.   When a file gets reasonably long, whenever it no longer can be listed on a single screen, you will begin to find it inconvenient to look for specific things in the file. For this reason, EDLIN provides a search command, S.

If you enter "S" or "s", followed by a string of characters, the first line in the file containing the string is displayed and made current. If the string isn't found, the current line remains as before. Let's look at an example. Here's our file:

```
 1:  One partridge in a pear tree
 2:  Two turtle doves
 3:  Three French hens
 4:  Four calling birds
 5:  Five golden rings
 6:*Six geese a-laying
 7:  Seven swans a-swimming
 8:  Eight maids a-milking
 9:  Nine ladies dancing
10:  Ten lords a-leaping
```

Rather than list the file to see which line contains "lords," you could enter this command:

```
*Slords
```

The result would be

```
10:*Ten lords a-leaping
*_
```

You could now edit that line by typing a period (.) and pressing Enter.

The string you enter must be exact, or you might find something you didn't want. Or you might get an error message.

```
*SLords
Not found
*_
```

Here, "Lords" with a capital "L" is not found in line 10, and so the string isn't found.

Here's another short file:

```
1:  The D command is entered
2:  to delete a line. It can be
3:  used to delete several lines,
4:*and it can be preceded by
5:  line numbers.
```

(a) What line is current after you use this command: *SLine _____

(b) What line is displayed and made current if you enter this command:

 *Sline _____

(c) What line is current after you use this command: *Suse _____

(d) Write a command to locate the first line containing "can".

 * _____

_ _ _ _ _ _ _ _ _ _ _

(a) 4 (unchanged; line is not found); (b) 2; (c) 3; (d) Scan or scan

7. Sometimes you are looking for a particular occurrence of a string. You don't necessarily want the first one. You can use a question mark (?) preceding "s". Then EDLIN will show you the line, and you can decide if you like it. If not, EDLIN shows you the next occurrence of the same string. Here's how such an interaction looks:

```
 1:  One partridge in a pear tree
 2:  Two turtle doves
 3:  Three French hens
 4:  Four calling birds
 5:  Five golden rings
 6:*Six geese a—laying
 7:  Seven swans a—swimming
 8:  Eight maids a—milking
 9:  Nine ladies dancing
10:  Ten lords a—leaping
*?sa—
 6:*Six geese a—laying
O.K.?n
 7: Seven swans a—swimming
O.K.?y
*
```

Now line 7 is current. The use of "?" causes the line containing the first occurrence of the string (a-) to be displayed, followed by the message, "O.K.?". You can enter "y" or just press Enter to accept the line. If you enter an "n", or anything else besides "y", EDLIN locates the line containing the next occurrence of the string, and you get a chance to accept it, as we did in the example above. After the last occurrence of the string is located and rejected, you'll get a "Not found" message.

Here's our other file again.

```
1:  The D command is entered
2:  to delete a line. It can be
3:  used to delete several lines,
4: *and it can be preceded by
5:  line numbers.
```

(a) What line will be displayed first if you enter this command:

?sbe _____

(b) The displayed line is followed by this line: O.K.? What is displayed next if you type "n" and press Enter?

_____

(c) What do you do to accept this line?

_____ A. Type "y" and press Enter

_____ B. Type "ok" and press Enter

_____ C. Just press Enter

(d) Write a command to display the line containing the first occurrence of "delete" and make it current.

_____

(e) Write a command to display the line containing the first occurrence of "delete." You want an opportunity to accept or reject this line. If you reject it, you want the line containing the next occurrence to be displayed for your

approval. _____

– – – – – – – – – – –

(a) 2; (b) line 4; (c) A or C; (d) sdelete (e) ?sdelete

8. When you use the search command without any preceding line numbers, the search begins at the first line of the file and continues through the last line if necessary. You can use beginning and ending line numbers to limit the search to a specific range. Here are two commands:

```
*6,12scan       *6,12?scan
```

Either of these commands will search for the first occurrence of the string "can" starting at line 6 and continuing through line 12. If the string isn't found within this range, the "Not found" message will be displayed. The ? has the same effect as before.

If you omit the first line number, the search will start with the first line in the file; so ,12srun will search lines 1 through 12 for the string "run." If you omit the second line number, the search will end with the last line in the file; so 12srun will cause a search from line 12 through the end of the file for the string "run."

Suppose you are editing a file that contains 288 lines. You want to look for the word INPUT.

(a) What command will show you the first occurrence in line 200 or later?

_____

(b) What command will show you the first occurrence in line 150 or later?

_____

(c) What command will let you check all occurrences of INPUT between lines 100 and 199?

_____

(d) What command will let you check all occurrences of INPUT in the file?

_____

— — — — — — — — — —

(a) 200sINPUT (b) 150sINPUT (c) 100,199?sINPUT (d) ?sINPUT

9. Before going on to the next command, let's take a moment to consider character strings, and what matches them. Suppose you have this command:

    *sbe< ↵ >.   (Enter immediately after *e*)

All the lines shown below match this string, because the two-character string "be" is included.

     6: I will be certain
     9: between the walls
    10: and between the rafters.
    13: cabel cars are rolling
    20: To be or not to be.
    32: That is not to be.
    42: He was a true Babe.
    45: A robe is a good coverup.

You could limit the matches by including a space in your character string.

Suppose you have this command:

    *s be<↵>   (space before b, Enter after e)

Now only these lines match:

     6: I will be certain
   10: and between the rafters.
   20: To be or not to be.
   32: That is not to be.

Suppose you have this command:

    *sbe <↵>   (space after e, before Enter)

Now these lines will be matched:

     6: I will be certain
   20: To be or not to be.
   45: A robe is a good coverup.

If you use this command;

    *s be <↵>   (a space before b and after e)

These lines will be matched:

     6: I will be certain
   20: To be or not to be.

You can see that spaces included in a character string are treated as characters. The string runs from the "s" to the carriage return produced when you press Enter.

(a) What command will show you every occurrence of the string "you" in a file?

    _____

(b) What command will show you occurrences of "you", except when it is not preceded by a space?

    _____

(c)   A file contains these words, and many others not similar to these.

```
appliance          plicate
appliances         plinth
pliable            duplicate
```

What search command will identify any one of these?

_____

(d)   Consider the list in question (c). What is the shortest command you could enter to select only the line that contains "pliable"?

_____

— — — — — — — — — —

(a) ?syou (b) ?s you (c) spli *or* ?spli (d) spliab *or* ?spliab

REPLACING CHARACTERS

10.   Frequently, you will not only want to locate a line that contains a character string, but also change that string to another one. For example, you may have used the word "lable" several times in a file. Then you recall that the correct spelling is "label." You could use the command "slable" to locate each occurrence, then edit the line and correct the spelling. However, EDLIN has another command that will accomplish the same thing more easily.

The R command is used to "replace" text. Here's an example:

rlable<F6>label<   >

As with the S command, the string begins immediately after the command letter. In the example, the string begins with "l". You use the F6 editing key on your monitor to mark the beginning of the replacement string. F6 shows up on your monitor as ^Z. Then you type the replacement string and press Enter. The example above will cause the entire file to be searched. Every occurrence of the string "lable" will be replaced by label. You'll see each line that is changed on the monitor. The last line that is changed is current when you see the EDLIN asterisk (*) prompt again. This is how it might appear on the console:

```
*rlable^Zlabel
     2: if there is no label, then
     8: all standard labels are
    12: when a user label is needed
    22: when the screen is scrollabel.
   *
```

Notice in the last case that "scrollable" is now misspelled!

(a) What EDLIN command can be used to locate a word and replace it with a different word? _____

(b) What DOS editing key do you use before entering a replacement string?

_____

(c) Write a command to replace all occurrences of "and" with "but".

_____

(d) Write a command to replace all occurrences of "observations" with "notes".

_____

(e) Write a command to replace all occurrences of "notes" with "observations".

_____

— — — — — — — — — — — —

(a) R (b) F6 (c) rand<F6>but (d) robservations<F6>notes (e) rnotes<F6>observations

11. The R command works much like S in terms of what lines are searched. That is, if you include two line numbers, the range of lines specified is searched and the replacement made. The command below causes lines 20 through 40 to be searched. Any occurrences of the string "0444" will be replaced by "0044".

```
    20,40 r0444<F6>0044
```

If you use just the first line number, all lines from that point to the end of the file are searched. If you use just the second line number, all lines from the start of the file to that line are searched. If you omit both line numbers, all lines in the file are searched for the first string.

Just as with the S command, you can use a question mark (?) to request a prompt each time the string is located. You will be shown the modified line and the O.K.? prompt. If you press "y" or Enter, the change is permanent. If you press anything else, the change is canceled and you see the next changed line. Here's how a sample interaction would look:

```
    *rand^Zbut
            2: boys, but girls may
    O.K.?y
            6: enter any commbuts they wish
    O.K.?n
           10: S but R formats
    O.K.?n
    *
```

Notice that "and" is changed to "but" even if it occurs in the middle of a word. This could have been avoided by including a space before and after "and" in the string.

(a) Write a command that will search the first 40 lines of a file, changing all occurrences of "INFILE" to "INPFILE". You don't want to verify each change.

(b) Write a command that will search lines 120 through the end of a file, changing occurrences of "OUTFILE" to "OFILE". You want to verify each change.

(c) You notice that you used the string "Wensday" in lines 40 through about 100 in a file. Write a command to correct it wherever it occurs.

(d) A file contains these lines:

```
1:  There is another way to solve the problem.
2:  If you enter not replacement string
3:  the first string will be deleted. There is not
4:  other way to delete a word without editing
5:  the line individually.
```

Notice that the word "not" is typed instead of "no" in two places. Write a command to correct this.

———————————————

(a) ,40rINFILE<F6>INPFILE (b) 120?rOUTFILE<F6>OFILE (c) 40,100rWensday<F6>Wednesday (be sure you used a capital W here) (d) ?rnot<F6>no (If you omit the ?, "another" will be changed to "anoher" in line 1 and you won't have a chance to reject it. If you include a space before or after "not", the two words will be changed effectively.)

12.   If you enter a search string (the first one) that doesn't exist in the file, you'll see the message "Not found". The current line won't change. If you omit the replacement string (following F6), the first string will be deleted from the file. Suppose this is a complete file:

```
1:  Many uses for PC EDLIN can be
2:  devised. You may want to
3:  create some new files to hold a
4:  summary of PC DOS commands.
5:  Or you may want to create
6:  a file of your checkbook register.
```

If you decide that "PC" is not really needed, you could use this command:

```
rPC <┘>
```

Notice the space following "PC". This will keep the spacing between words consistent. If you just deleted "PC", two spaces (the one before and after "PC") would appear where the deletion was made.

When you omit the replacement string, you are in effect telling EDLIN to replace the search string with nothing; the result is to delete the search string. It's a good idea to use the ? when deleting strings in this way, so you don't delete anything you didn't intend to.

(a)   Suppose you enter this command for the above file:

```
?rdeviced<F6>devised
```

What will be displayed?

_____ A.   2: deviced. You may want to

_____ B.   2: devised. You may want to

_____ C.   O.K.?

_____ D.   Not found.

(b) Suppose you enter this command for the above file:

   ?rfile<F6>listing

   What will be displayed?

   _____ A.   3: create some new files to hold a

   _____ B.   3: create some new files to hold a

        O.K.?

   _____ C.   3: create some new listings to hold a

   _____ D.   3: create some new listings to hold a

        O.K.?

(c) Write a command to delete all occurrences of the word "may".

   _____

(d) Write a command to delete the word "some" from line 3.

   _____

- - - - - - - - - -

(a) D; (b) D; (c) rmay <↵> (d) 3,3rsome <↵>

13.   You have seen now how to use the search (S) and replace (R) commands for
EDLIN. Let's compare the two as a review before going on to another topic. Write
the name of the command (S, R, both, or neither) each of the following indicates.

(a) Will show you the first occurrence of a given string _____

(b) Will change a string to another one _____

(c) Can be used to delete a string _____

(d) Can be used with ? to allow you to reject a line _____

(e) May affect which line is current _____

- - - - - - - - - -

(a) s; (b) r; (c) r; (d) both; (e) both (If the "Not found" message is displayed, then
the current line isn't changed. Otherwise, it is.)

LONGER FILES

Up to now, we have been assuming that the files we used under EDLIN fit entirely in memory. EDLIN can operate only on lines that are in memory; so if a file contains more lines than can fit in memory at a given time, you need to use special techniques to move parts of the file into and out of memory. In this section, you'll learn to handle such files.

14. When you begin to edit a new file, you see the message "New file". When you begin to edit an existing file, it is first read into memory until memory is about 75 percent full. If the file fits into memory, you'll see the message "End of input file". Let's assume you have a 64K system. About 500 lines of no more than 75 characters each will fit in memory at one time. If you begin to edit a file that contains 600 or 700 lines, you'll see no message.

```
A>EDLIN B:BIG
*
```

This means that lines from the file have been read into memory, which is now about 75 percent full. This allows a good amount of space for inserting new lines, which you can do up to 100 percent of memory. As usual, the lines in memory are numbered from 1 through the largest number. At this point, you can use any or all of the EDLIN commands you have learned up to now.

If you want to find out how many lines are in memory, you can use an insert command. Here's an example:

```
A>EDLIN B:BIG
*#i
     362:*
```

The command #i says you want to insert lines after the last line in memory. EDLIN gives you line number 362. This tells you that memory contains lines 1 through 361. You can use Ctrl-Break to cancel insert mode. When you are working with large files, it's a good idea to check the highest line number.

(a) Identify the interaction on the right that represents beginning to edit each file on the left.

_____ A.   A file that did not exist

_____ B.   A file that contains 80 lines

_____ C.   A file that contains 800 lines

1.   A>edlin one
     *

2.   A>edlin two
     New file
     *_

3.   A>edlin three
     End of input file
     *_

(b) When you begin to edit a very large file, what percentage of available memory is filled with lines? _____

(c) What command can you use to identify the number of the last line in memory? _____

_ _ _ _ _ _ _ _ _ _ _ _

(a) A–2; B–3; C–1; (b) 75% (about); (c) #i

15. The first part of a long file is automatically read into memory by the EDLIN command. You edit this part as if it were a shorter file. Then you need to move on.

EDLIN has two commands you need to use to edit later parts of the file. First you use the write command (W) to write lines from memory to the edit file. Lines beginning with line 1 are written to the $$$ file that was created when you entered EDLIN. Suppose you discover with #i that memory contains 361 lines. You haven't inserted any lines. You could use the command "361W"; this causes the 361 lines, in their current edited form, to be written to the edit file. They are no longer in memory, and so you can't change them. If you enter the command "i" now, you can add lines after 361. If you used "150W", then the first 150 lines in memory would be written to the file. The remaining lines in memory would be renumbered starting with 1 up to 161. If you don't specify a number in a write command, lines are written only until memory is again 75 percent full of lines.

Suppose you are editing a very large file, and you have had this interaction;

```
A>EDLIN DATA.XXX
*#i
        427:*^C
*
```

(a) What command would put the first 300 of those lines on the disk? _____

(b) What command would put the remaining lines on the disk?

_____

(c) Suppose you just had the interaction above, followed by this:

```
*300i
        300:*New line
        301:*New line
        302:*New line
        303:*New line
        304:*^C
```

What command will write the complete set of lines in memory to the disk?

_____

(d) Suppose you have just had the interaction shown in (c), except you added 100 lines. What command would write lines to disk until memory is only 75 percent full? _____

_ _ _ _ _ _ _ _ _ _

(a) 300W (b) 126W (c) 430W (d) W

16. Once lines are written from a file to memory, those lines are no longer in memory. You can now use the append (A) command to read more lines from the file into memory. The lines that are read in begin with the line following the last one read by EDLIN or another A command. If you use "A" without any line number, lines will be read into memory until it is 75 percent full, just as at the beginning of EDLIN. If you do specify a number, that number of lines will be read into memory, as long as there is room.

Let's continue the earlier example:

```
A>EDLIN DATA.XXX
*#i
        427:*^C
*426W
*a
End of input file
*#i
        326:*
```

Now the $$$ file contains the first 426 lines from the original file; you can't go back and edit them without restarting EDLIN. The next 325 lines have been appended into memory. The message "End of input file" indicates that the entire file has now been read in. The file contains 751 lines (426 + 325). You are now set up to edit the last 325 of them.

Suppose you have had this interaction:

```
A>EDLIN DATA.XXX
*#i
        427:*^C
*_
```

You want to be able to edit lines 200 through 500 (that's 301 lines) in the original file.

(a) What command would you use so that the first line in *memory* is the 200th line of the file? _____

(b) What file lines are now contained in memory? _____

(c) What command would you use to put the rest of the lines, up through file line 500, in *memory*? _____

(d) Now suppose you are finished editing those lines. How can you store them all on disk? _____

(e) How can you fill memory (up to 75%) with more lines?

_____

(f) What message will you see when the last part of the file is read into memory?

_____

— — — — — — — — — — —

(a) 199W (b) 200 through 426 in the original file; (c) 74a (d) 301W (e) a (f) End of input file

17.   When you are inserting lines into a file, either a new file or an existing one, you can fill memory completely. When you do, you'll be removed from insert mode and see a "Memory full" message. If you have more lines to add, you write some existing lines to disk, invoke insert mode again, and continue entering lines into memory.

Let's look at an example.

Enter new long file:

```
A>EDLIN B:DATA.FIL
New file
*i
        1: (enter hundreds of short lines)
Memory full
*500W
*i
        1: (enter hundreds more)
Memory full
*500W
i
        1: (enter a few more)^C
*48W
```

end edit

```
*e
```

start again

```
A>EDLIN B:DATA.FIL
```

memory is 75% full
```
*
```

Now you can use any or all of the EDLIN commands to edit your file, even insert. When you're finished, use a write command.

```
*487W
```

Append the next batch of lines until memory is 75% full.

```
*a
```

Now you can edit these
```
*
```

Notice that you cannot go backwards in appending lines to memory. Once the first part of the file has been written to the $$$ file, you must leave EDLIN and invoke it again to edit the early lines.

Write the command you would use for each task below.

(a) Begin to edit a file named COLOSSUS that contains 2000 lines. _____

(b) Write 458 lines to the $$$ file. _____

(c) Memory contains 458 lines. Write them all to disk. _____

(d) Memory contains lines 1 through 412. Write lines 1 to 200 to disk. _____

(e) Memory contains lines 1 through 412. Write lines 201 to 412 to disk. ___

(f) Read 200 lines from the disk into memory. _____

(g) Read lines into memory until it is 75% full. _____

— — — — — — — — —

(a) EDLIN COLOSSUS (b) 458W (c) 458W (not just "W") (d) 200W (e) can't, you
could do 412W, but that writes all 412; (f) 200a (g) a

18.   To terminate editing of a large file, you use Q or E just as with shorter files.
The Q command will erase the $$$ file and leave you with your original file,
unchanged. The E command will cause any remaining lines to be written to the
$$$ file. Then the original file will be renamed with the BAK extension. The $$$
file will be renamed, as you specified in the EDLIN command. If you want to
change only the first line in a 60K file, you might have this interaction:

```
A>EDLIN CHAPTER3.NEW
*1
    1:*             CHAPTER 3 THE DEVELOPER
    1:*_
```

You make your changes, then press Enter. Memory is 75 percent full of lines.
When you enter the E command, these lines are written to the $$$ file. Then the
rest of the lines in the CHAPTER3.NEW file are written to CHAPTER3.$$$. Then
the names are changed.

A file can get too large to be edited. The maximum size of a file is limited by the
amount of space on a disk. Theoretically, a disk that holds 160K bytes will hold a
file of up to 160K characters. But you can't edit a file that large. A file of 80K
characters can be edited, but you probably couldn't insert too many extra lines. If
a disk contains other files as well, you'll have to have a smaller limit for an
editable file.

The general rule is that you need at least as much free space on the disk as your
file occupies. The BAK file that is erased may free up the space you need.

(a) What DOS command would you use to find how much free space is available on a disk? _____

(b) What DOS command would you use to find how much space a particular file occupies? _____

(c) Suppose ED1.C contains 40K bytes. ED1.BAK contains 30K bytes. The disk has 20K bytes available.

    A.   Can you safely edit ED1.C? _____

    B.   Can you double the size of ED1.C with inserted lines?

    _____

(d) Suppose ED2.D contains 40K bytes. ED2.BAK contains 10K bytes. The disk has 20K bytes available.

    A.   Can you safely edit ED2.D? _____

    B.   If so, can you double its size? _____

    C.   If not, what could you do to edit ED2.D?_____

    _____

    _____

(e) Suppose you have edited ED1.C including inserting some lines. The console shows this:

```
    *A
    *rDIVISION^ZDIVISION
         193:              PROCEDURE DIVISION.
    *
```

You want to end editing and store the changed file, even though all lines have not yet been read into memory. What is the quickest valid way?

_____ A. Press Enter

_____ B. Type E and press Enter

_____ C. Type Q and press Enter

_____ D. Use W and A commands until all lines have been appended; then use the E command

----

(a) CHKDISK; (b) DIR; (c) A—yes, B—no (you have 50K bytes for a new version of a 40K byte file); (d) A—no (You have 30K bytes for changes to a 40K file), B—can't, C—copy it to a less full disk, or erase files from that disk; (e) B

You have seen how you can create or edit a long file by handling it one piece at a time in memory. You use the "W" command to write edited lines to disk, then the "A" command to place more unedited lines in memory. You can use all the EDLIN commands and the DOS editing keys on whatever lines are in memory.

Chapter Ten Self-Test

1. What is the maximum length for an editable line under EDLIN? _____

2. Suppose you list three lines that are each about 200 characters long. You have pressed Ctrl-PrtSc. Your printer is set for 80-character lines.

    a. Is the listing readable on the console? _____

    b. Is the listing readable on the printer? _____

3. Suppose you have listed three lines (each about 200 characters long) on the console. Then you press Shift-PrtScr. Is the listing readable on the printer?

    _____

4. Suppose you have a file that contains six lines. You want to repeat line 6 before the first line.

    a. How can you put the contents of line 6 in the input buffer?

    Step 1: _____

    Step 2: _____

    b. How can you use it before line 1?

    Step 1: _____

    Step 2: _____

5. Write a command to eliminate line 7 from a file. _____

6. Write a command to eliminate the string "linear" from a file wherever it occurs. _____

7. Write a command to eliminate all lines from the current line (47) through line 180. _____

8. Write a command to eliminate all lines from line 12 through the current line (47). _____

9. Line 47 is current. You want to delete line 38. You enter "d38". What line is deleted? _____

10. Write a command that will cause the first line in the file that contains the string "prepare" to be displayed and made current.

    _____

11. A file contains 250 lines. Write a command that will show you, one at a time, all lines that contain "COBOL" in the first half of the file. _____

12. A file contains 250 lines. Write a command that will show you the first occurrence, if any, of "DIVISION" between lines 100 and 200. _____

13. Write a command that will cause all occurrences of "Enviroment" or "enviroment" to be changed to "Environment" or "environment." You don't want to verify each change. _____

14. Write a command that will change the word "monkey" to "ape" in lines 200 through the end of the file. You want to approve each change. _____

15. Name the EDLIN command you would use for each of these:

    a. Display a line containing a given character string _____

    b. Eliminate six adjacent lines from a file _____

    c. Change one word to another in part of the file _____

    d. Copy lines from memory to a $$$ file on disk _____

    e. Copy lines from the file being edited to memory _____

16. Suppose you have been entering lines and the console looks like this:

                718: BALL, BLUE, 12
        Memory full
        *_

    You have more lines to enter. What command do you use here?

    * _____

17. You have this interaction on your console:

        A>EDLIN SELF.TST
        *

    a. Is the entire file in memory? _____

    b. How much of memory is full? _____

    c. What command will let you know how many lines are in memory?

        _____

18. You have 361 lines in memory.

    a. What command will store the first 160 on disk? _____

b. What command would store them all on disk? _____

c. What command would read 100 lines from the file and put them into memory? _____

d. What command would fill memory 75% with lines from the file? ___

19. You need to create a file that will eventually be 40K bytes long.

a. What command will tell you how much space is available on the disk?

_____

b. You will be repeatedly editing this file. How much disk space will you need? _____

Self-Test Answer Key

1. 253 characters (254 can be stored, but you can't edit this line)
2. a. yes
    b. no
3. Yes
4. a. 6, then Ctrl-Break
    b. 1i, then F3
5. 7d
6. slinear or ?slinear
7. ,180d (or 47,180d)
8. 12,47d (not 12d)
9. 47
10. sprepare
11. ,125?sCOBOL
12. 100,200sDIVISION
13. rnviroment<F6>nvironment
14. 200?rmonkey<F6>ape
15. a. S
    b. D
    c. R
    d. W
    e. A
16. 718W

17. a. No
    b. 75%
    c. #i
18. a. 160W
    b. 361W
    c. 100a
    d. a
19. a. CHKDISK
    b. 80K

Suggested Machine Exercise

Part I

1. Boot your system and call up your file ED1.ME for more editing. The file should look like this:

```
1: EDITED FILE
2:
3: This is the very first file I have edited.
4:
5: In the process, I've used several different
6: editing commands, including I and E.
7: When I finished, I stored
8: the entire file on disk.
9: The DOS editing keys are useful.
```

2. Repeat line 9 ten more times.

3. Add a new last line: "This is an experiment to see how a very long line will look on the console and on the printer. It should be long enough." Repeat this line three times.

4. Your file should contain 20 lines. List the entire file on the console and the printer (use Ctrl-PrtSc). Examine the print output.

5. Use Shift-PrtSc to print the screen. Compare this printout to the earlier one.

6. Eliminate line 4.

7. Eliminate the last nine copies of "The DOS editing keys are useful."

8. Eliminate all but one copy of the long line.

9. Have EDLIN show you the first occurrence of "edit". Then have it show you all occurrences.

10. Have EDLIN change "I" as a separate word to "you" wherever it occurs. Do not change the command I to "you".

11. Practice more with the D, S, and R commands until you feel comfortable with them.

Part II

If you'll be working with long files, take time to create one now for practice.

1. Build a long file. Work on a disk with at least 80K available space. Here's how you can do it easily:
    a. Enter a long line (about 100 to 120 characters for line 1) Include "line 1" in the line. Press Enter.

b. Press F3 and then Enter.

c. Repeat step b until you reach line 100.

d. Use DOS editing keys to repeat the same line with "line 100" in place of "line 1". Press Enter.

e. Press F3; then Enter.

f. Repeat step e until you reach line 200.

g. Continue until you have about 600 lines. The flagged lines at the hundred markers will help you locate those lines later.

2. Store the file.

3. Edit the file.

a. Notice that the message does *not* say "End of input file".

b. Check what the last line number in memory is.

c. Locate your "hundred markers."

d. Now store those lines on disk and read in the next section. Check the "hundred markers."

e. If you haven't seen "End of input file" yet, repeat step d.

4. You can erase this file after the exercise if you wish.

CHAPTER ELEVEN
Batch Processing

You can submit a batch of DOS commands at one time by placing them in a BAT file and asking DOS to execute the BAT file. You will learn how to do that in this chapter.

When you have finished this chapter, you will be able to:

- Create a BAT file
- Code the PAUSE command
- Code the REM command
- Code dummy parameters
- Execute a BAT file
- Supply dummy parameters
- Respond to PAUSE commands
- Abort a batch run
- Create an AUTOEXEC.BAT file
- Interpret error messages associated with batch files

WHAT IS A BATCH FILE?

1. A batch file is a file with extension BAT that contains one or more DOS commands. For example, here is a file to format and then check a disk. The filename is NEWDISK.BAT.

```
FORMAT/S B:
CHKDSK B:
```

To execute this batch file, we enter this:

```
A>NEWDISK
```

The response will look like this:

```
A>format/s b:
Insert new diskette for drive B:
and strike any key when ready

Formatting . . . Format complete
System transferred

    160256   bytes total disk space
     13824   bytes used by system
    146432   bytes available on disk

Format another (Y/N)?n
A>chkdsk b:

    160256   bytes total disk space
      8704   bytes in 2 hidden files
      5120   bytes in 1 user files
    146432   bytes available on disk

     65536   bytes total memory
     53136   bytes free
```

As the batch was executed, we had to respond to directions such as ". . . strike any key when ready" and questions such as "Format another (Y/N)?" just as we do when we run these commands individually.

Using batch files keeps you from having to type and retype commands that you use a lot. For example, suppose you want to make vault copies of 20 disks. Rather than enter the DISKCOPY and DISKCOMP commands 20 times, you can prepare a BAT file and just execute it 20 times.

(a) What does a batch file contain?

_____

(b) How are batch files used?

_____ A. To keep all the DOS external commands together on a disk

_____ B. To run long jobs without having to respond to questions and directions

_____ C. To avoid having to retype the commands in frequently used operations

— — — — — — — — — —

(a) DOS commands; (b) C

2. To create a batch file, simply use COPY or EDLIN to make a file containing the DOS commands you want to use. There are also some special batch commands which you will learn later in this chapter.

You can refer to another batch file as the last command in your file.

The file should be named with the extension BAT. Since the filename (without the extension) will be used as a command, it should not duplicate any of the internal commands nor any of the external commands that are on the same disk.

(a) Which of the following are good batch file identifiers?

    ____ A.   FREE.BAT   ____ D.   TYPE.BAT

    ____ B.   NEW.COM   ____ E.   HOLD.BAT

    ____ C.   LEXT   ____ F.   MERGE.DOC

(b) Code the contents of a batch file which will copy all the nonsystem files except COM, BAS, and EXE files, from drive A to drive B.

(c) What might you call the above file?_____

(d) True or false? External commands cannot be used as batch file names. _

(e) True or false? One batch file cannot refer to another batch file. ____

__ __ __ __ __ __ __ __ __ __

(a) A and E [B, C, and F don't end with .BAT, and D uses an internal command as the filename]

(b) COPY *.* B:
ERASE B:*.COM
ERASE B:*.BAS
ERASE B:*.EXE

(c) We'd call it COPYTEXT.BAT or COPYASCI.BAT; (d) false—you can use an external command as long as its COM file is not on the same disk (but you probably shouldn't, it's too confusing); (e) False—one batch file can execute another batch file, but only as the last command.

EXECUTING BATCH JOBS

3. To execute a batch file, simply enter the filename without the extension. Of course, the BAT file must be on the drive you specify. For example, suppose drive A contains MERGE.BAT. To execute that file, you would enter:

A>MERGE

If MERGE.BAT is on drive B rather than drive A, you could enter:

A>B:MERGE

If the DOS programs being executed require individual responses, you'll have to enter them as usual. You can't build them into the batch file. Suppose you execute MAKECOPY.BAT, which contains these commands:

DIR/P B:
ERASE B:*.*
COPY *.* B:

First, the initial page of the directory of the disk in B is displayed. The system then pauses and waits for you to strike any key. You must continue to strike keys until the directory finishes. Next you will see:

A>ERASE B:*.*
Are you sure (Y/N)?_

You must respond to this question before the batch job will continue. After the erasure takes place, the copies will be made automatically.

Suppose A disk contains SECOND.BAT and HALF.BAT, and B disk contains THRU.BAT.

(a) Code a command to execute SECOND.BAT.

A>_____

(b) Code a command to execute THRU.BAT.

A>_____

(c) Which of the following statements is true.

_____ A. You must respond to questions and directions just as if you were entering the commands one at a time.

_____ B. With batch jobs, you don't need to respond to questions and directions.

— — — — — — — — — —

(a) A>SECOND; (b) B:THRU; (c) A

4. You can use several of the control functions while a batch job is running. You can echo print, suspend the job, and cancel the current command or the job. To cancel, you press Ctrl-Break. DOS will ask you this question:

```
Terminate batch job (Y/N)?
```

You have to differentiate between the current command and the whole job. If you want only the current command to be terminated, enter N. If you want the whole batch job to be terminated, enter Y.

Suppose you are running a batch job called TYPALL.

(a) How can you suspend the job long enough to look at the current display?

_____

(b) Suppose currently the command TYPE FIRST is executing. How can you cancel the command and go on to the next command in the batch?

_____

What do you enter after "Terminate batch job (Y/N)?"_____

(c) Suppose you want to cancel the entire batch job. What keys do you press?

_____

What do you enter after "Terminate batch job (Y/N)?" _____

_ _ _ _ _ _ _ _ _ _

(a) Ctrl-NumLock; (b) press Ctrl-Break; N; (c) Ctrl-Break; Y

5. Here are a few sample batch job requests showing some of the messages you can get.

```
A>loaddisk
Bad command or file name
```

Here the LOADDISK.BAT job is not on the default drive.

```
A>compdisk

A>diskcomp a: b:

Insert first diskette in drive A:

Insert second diskette in drive B:

Strike any key when ready

Comparing 1 side(s)

Compare error(s) on
Track 00, Side 0

Compare error(s) on
Track 01, Side 0

Compare error(s) on
Track 02, Side 0

C^C

Terminate batch job (Y/N)? n
A>
Insert disk with batch file
and strike any key when ready

A>chkdsk b:

        160256   bytes total disk space
          8704   bytes in 2 hidden files
          5120   bytes in 1 user files
        146432   bytes available on disk

         65536   bytes total memory
         53136   bytes free

A>
```

Here we terminated the first command when we realized that we had installed the wrong two disks. Because we had changed the disk in drive A, DOS couldn't find the COMPDISK.BAT file when it wanted to, and so it asked for the disk containing the batch file again. We reloaded the file containing COMPDISK.BAT and pressed a character key.

You can also get the usual error messages associated with each of the individual commands. For example, if you try to execute an external command whose COM file is not on the proper disk, you'll get this message:

```
Bad command or filename
```

(a) Suppose you run a batch job that involves removing the disk containing the batch file. When you see this message:

```
Insert disk with batch file
and strike any key when ready_
```

What should you do?

_____ A. Put any DOS disk in drive A and hit a character key.

_____ B. Put a disk containing the batch file in drive A and hit a character key.

_____ C. Put any disk in drive A and hit a character key.

(b) Suppose you have this interaction:

```
A>COMPRESS
Bad command or file name
A>_
```

What's wrong?

_____ A. There's no COMPRESS.COM or COMPRESS.EXE file on drive A.

_____ B. There's no internal command called COMPRESS.

_____ C. There's no COMPRESS.BAT file on drive A.

_____ D. All of the above.

(c) Suppose you have this interaction:

```
A>COMPRESS
A>FORMAT B:
Bad command or file name
```

What's wrong?

_____ A. There's no COMPRESS.BAT file on drive A.

_____ B. You can't reference an external command from a batch file.

_____ C. There's no FORMAT.COM file on drive A.

_____ D. All of the above.

— — — — — — — — — —

(a) B; (b) D; (c) C

    DOS includes four special facilities to be used with batch jobs—the REM command, the PAUSE command, the AUTOEXEC.BAT file, and dummy parameters. The remainder of this chapter will deal with these four facilities.

THE REM COMMAND

6.   REM is a special command that can be used in batch files. It stands for "remarks." It causes a remark, or comment, to be displayed on the console when it is processed. No other action takes place.
    Here is an example of a batch file containing REM commands:

```
REM THIS JOB FORMATS THE DISK ON B *WITH* THE
REM DOS SYSTEM FILES. IF YOU DON'T WANT THE SYSTEM
REM FILES, USE "NEWDISKN" INSTEAD.
FORMAT/S B:
CHKDSK B:
```

    When we execute this job, we can use Ctrl-Break to terminate the job after the first message of the FORMAT command if we want to switch to NEWDISKN.

Here is what happens when we execute this file as a batch job:

```
A>NEWDISK
A>REM THIS JOB FORMATS THE DISK ON B *WITH* THE
A>REM DOS SYSTEM FILES. IF YOU DON'T WANT THE SYSTEM
A>REM FILES, USE "NEWDISKN" INSTEAD.

A>FORMAT/S B:
Insert new diskette for drive B:
and strike any key when ready

Formatting . . . Format complete
System transferred

      160256   bytes total disk space
       13824   bytes used by system
      146432   bytes available on disk

Format another (Y/N)?n
A>CHKDSK B:

      160256   bytes total disk space
        8704   bytes in 2 hidden files
        5120   bytes in 1 user files
      146432   bytes available on disk

       65536   bytes total memory
       53136   bytes free

A>_
```

Remarks help to document your batch jobs. This is especially helpful for jobs that other people will use or that you yourself will use only once in a while. Each REM line can be up to 123 characters long.

Add a comment to the following file to remind the user that it can be used only on disks that have already been formatted with room to hold the system files.

```
SYS B:
CHKDSK B:
DIR B:
```

————————————

Here's our solution. Yours is probably worded differently:

```
REM THIS JOB USES THE SYS COMMAND, WHICH REQUIRES A DISK IN DRIVE B
THAT HAS BEEN FORMATTED WITH ROOM FOR THE SYSTEM FILES.
```

THE PAUSE COMMAND

7. You know that some DOS commands will ask you to do something, then wait for a response. You can make your batch jobs do the same thing by coding the PAUSE command.

If you code PAUSE with no operand, it will cause the system to display this message:

```
Strike a key when ready . . .
```

then wait for the user to respond.

If you put a comment after PAUSE, the comment will be displayed before the "Strike a key" message. Thus, if you code PAUSE PLEASE SWITCH THE DISK IN DRIVE B, the user will see:

```
PLEASE SWITCH THE DISK IN DRIVE B
Strike a key when ready . . .
```

The comment may be up to 121 bytes long.

(a) Add a line to the following job that will give the user a chance to put the appropriate disk in drive B before the CHKDSK program begins.

```
CHKDSK B:
DIR B:
```

(b) *Extra thought question:* Why do you think a REM comment can be 123 characters but a PAUSE comment can be only 121 characters?

_____

_____

(c) If you wanted to have more than 121 characters as a comment before a pause, what would you do?

_____

_____

— — — — — — — — — — —

(a) PAUSE PUT THE DISK TO BE CHECKED IN DRIVE B (b) the maximum DOS command length is 126 characters; "REM" takes up three characters, leaving 123, while "PAUSE" takes up five characters, leaving 121; (c) code REM commands before the PAUSE command (don't code multiple PAUSE commands unless you want the system to stop after each one)

THE AUTOEXEC.BAT FACILITY

8.   When you boot DOS, the DATE and TIME commands are automatically executed. But you can set up DOS disks to substitute other commands for DATE and TIME. All you need to do is place a file named AUTOEXEC.BAT on any disk where you want to control the initial commands that are executed.

For example, suppose you want to establish a standard of always making a vault copy of the boot disk at the beginning of each session, before you begin to update files and add files to that disk. You could put the following AUTOEXEC.BAT file on every boot disk.

```
PAUSE Please install vault disk in drive B
DISKCOPY A: B:
PAUSE Boot disk vaulted. Please remove and save.
REM Don't forget to update the DATE and TIME.
```

(a)   Create a file that will cause the directories of the A and B drives to be displayed every time the system is booted from this disk. Then do the date and time functions.

(b)   What will you name the above file?_____

— — — — — — — — — — —

(a)   DIR A:
DIR B:
DATE
TIME

(b)   AUTOEXEC.BAT

USING DUMMY PARAMETERS

9.   You can code a batch file to receive parameters when it is executed. To do this, you put dummy parameters in the file. The dummy parameters are %0, %1, %2, . . ., %9. Use them in place of command parameters such as filenames and drivenames.

For example, suppose you want to set up a batch job to copy and compare a file of any name. You can code the job this way:

```
COPY %1 %2
COMP %1 %2
```

To execute this command, you enter the BAT filename followed by a value for %1 and a value for %2, like this:

```
A>COPYFILE NEWJOB B:
```

DOS will substitute the first parameter for all occurences of %1 in the batch file. The second parameter is substituted for all occurences of %2. Thus, the job that will be executed in our example becomes:

```
COPY NEWJOB B:
COMP NEWJOB B:
```

(a) Suppose we decide to use COPYFILE again, this time entering A>COPYFILE DOLLARS CENTS. Write out the job that will be executed.

(b) Code a command to use COPYFILE to copy and verify QUESTB, from drive B, as ANSB, on drive A.

A>_____

— — — — — — — — — — —

(a) COPY DOLLARS CENTS
    COMP DOLLARS CENTS
(b) A>COPYFILE B:QUESTB ANSB

10. When you enter a batch command, the dummy parameters are always lined up with the parts of the command this way:

```
        %0          %1        %2        %3       %4    . . .
   A>NEWFILE    TWOFORD   B:AXLES   B:DRAPE   B:     . . .
```

Thus, the %0 parameter, if used, always refers to the command name itself. %1 always refers to the first operand, %2 to the second operand, and so on.

You will rarely, if ever, use %0 in a batch file. If you use dummy parameters at all, you'll start with %1. It makes no sense to skip %1 and start with %2 or a higher parameter, because it would be very awkward to code the command to execute the job. So always use the dummy parameters in order, except that you can skip %0.

(a) The %0 parameter always refers to _____

In this command:

```
A>GETFILE B:DOLLARS B:CENTS
```

(b)   What value will be used for %1? _____

(c)   What value will be used for %2? _____

(d)   Here is an incorrectly coded BAT file:

```
COPY %4 + %5 + %6 %9
TYPE %9
```

What is wrong with this file?

_____

— — — — — — — — — —

(a) the command name; (b) B:DOLLARS; (c) B:CENTS; (d) it should use %1 to %4, not %4, %5, %6, and %9

11.   In a batch file, you can use a dummy parameter for any operand or any part of an operand. You can also use a dummy parameter for the command name. The following job is a little silly, but it demonstrates the possible ways to use dummy parameters.

```
FORMAT %1
COPY *.%2 %1
COPY %3.COM %1
%4 %1
DIR %5 %1
```

Now suppose we want to run this job on the disk in drive B, copying *.DAT and C*.COM to that disk and then checking the disk and printing its directory using pause mode. Here's the command we would enter:

```
A>PREPDISK B: DAT C* CHKDSK /P
```

Which of the following BAT lines are legal?

_____ (a) TYPE %2:%1

_____ (b) DIR/%2 %1:

_____ (c) COPY %0.BAT B:

_____ (d) %1 B:

— — — — — — — — — —

They are all legal

12. If you leave out a parameter when you execute a batch job, that parameter will be replaced with a null value in the file. When you enter a batch command, you can leave out only the parameters at the end. You can't leave out parameters in the middle since DOS counts them from left to right.

Suppose the DUP.BAT file contains these commands:

```
COPY %3%1 %4%2
COMP %3%1 %4%2
TYPE %4%2
```

Suppose you enter this command:

```
A>DUP XFILE YFILE A: A:
```

Here's what will be executed:

```
COPY A:XFILE A:YFILE
COMP A:XFILE A:YFILE
TYPE A:YFILE
```

Now suppose we enter this command:

```
A>DUP XFILE ZFILE
```

Here's what will be executed:

```
COPY XFILE ZFILE
COMP XFILE ZFILE
TYPE ZFILE
```

Suppose the D.BAT file contains this command:

```
DIR %1 %2
```

(a) Code a D command to get a wide directory of drive B.

A>_____

(b) Code a D command to get a normal directory of drive B.

A>_____

(c) Code a D command to get a normal directory of the default drive.

A>_____

— — — — — — — — — —

(a) D /W B: (b) D B: (c) D

Chapter Eleven Self-Test

1. Which of the following are good names for batch files?
   a. LAST.COM   d. TWOCOPY.BAT   g. COPY.COM
   b. SEND   e. LIFT.DOC   h. CLEAR.BAT
   c. DATE.BAT   f. LEFTHAND   i. PUSHER.ZON

2. What must you name a file that should be executed as part of the booting

   procedure?_____

3. Code a batch file that will erase all the files on drive B, and then display the
   status of that drive.

4. What will you name the above file?_____

5. Code a command to execute the above file.

   A>_____

6. Code a batch file to erase files from disk B, with the file identifier to be
   supplied when the batch job is executed. Display the directory of B after the
   files have been erased.

7. Give a name to the above batch file._____

8. Use your batch file to erase all the files with extension BAK from the disk.

   A>_____

9. Use your batch file to erase B:LOCKOUT.COM.

   A>_____

10. Change your batch job from question 7 so that the drivename can also be
    specified at execution time. Also, add remarks at the beginning to explain
    what the job does.

11. Now execute the job to erase all files starting with PERT on drive B.

    A>_____

12. Execute the job to erase all files with extension MAX on drive A.

    A>_____

13. Code a batch file that does three disk checks in a row, giving the user a chance to change the disk in drive B before every one.

14. What does this message mean:

    ```
    Insert disk with batch file
    and strike any key when ready_
    ```

    a. The system wants to reboot itself and needs a DOS disk to do so.
    b. DOS wants to copy the system files from drive A to B.
    c. DOS is ready to execute the next command in the batch file and can't find the batch file on drive A.

15. Suppose you want to abort the current command in a batch job without aborting the whole job. What do you do?

    _____

16. Suppose you want to abort an entire batch job. What do you do?

    _____

Self-Test Answer Key

1. d and h
2. AUTOEXEC.BAT
3. ERASE B:*.*
    CHKDSK B:
4. In our examples, we'll call it CLEARB.BAT.
5. A>CLEARB

6. ERASE B:%1
   DIR B:

7. In our examples, we'll call it DELB.BAT.

8. A>DELB *.BAK

9. A>DELB LOCKOUT.COM

10. REM: This erases the specified files from the specified drive and then displays the directory of that drive.
    ERASE %1%2
    DIR %1

11. A>DELB B: PERT*.*

12. A>DELB A: *.MAX

13. PAUSE   Put the first disk in drive B
    CHKDSK B:
    PAUSE   Change the disk in drive B
    CHKDSK B:
    PAUSE   Change the disk in drive B
    CHKDSK B:

14. c

15. Press Ctrl-Break; answer N to the question

16. Press Ctrl-Break; answer Y to the question

Suggested Machine Exercise

In this machine exercise, you will create and use several batch jobs.

1. Boot DOS.
2. Using EDLIN, create a batch file to do a disk check of drive A, then display a directory of that drive. Put lots of remarks in your file.
3. Run your batch file. (Correct it if it doesn't work properly.)
4. Run your job again. Try aborting it during the first command.
5. Change your batch job so it gives you a chance to change the disk in drive A before the CHKDSK command.
6. Run the new version of the batch job. If you change the disk, what happens? After the PAUSE command is processed, DOS needs the BAT file back again to find the next command, and so changing the disk does no good.
7. Change your batch job so you can enter the drivename when you execute the file.
8. Now execute the file again, this time for drive B, if you have one.
9. Create an AUTOEXEC.BAT file that will display these remarks:

```
HI. WELCOME TO THE IBM PERSONAL
COMPUTER. DON'T FORGET TO SET THE
DATE AND TIME.
```

10. Now reboot with your disk and watch what happens.

This completes your course on using the Personal Computer DOS. You have learned the details of all the internal commands and those external commands used by nonprogrammers. If you have done all the machine exercises, you should feel pretty comfortable with using these commands and interpreting their messages. We hope you enjoy using your Personal Computer. If you want to learn even more about it, you will find the books listed in the front of this book useful.

Index

Arrows, in EDLIN, 161
ASCII files, binary files and, 93
Asterisk, 69, 70, 71
   in EDLIN, 141–142, 158
   in global file identifiers, 73–74
AUTOEXEC.BAT facility, batch
     processing and, 213

Backspace key, 39
Backup copy, *see* Copy Command
Bad disks, 114–115
BAS, 68
Batch file, defined, 203–205
Batch processing, 203–220
   and AUTOEXEC.BAT facility,
     213
   dummy parameters for, 213–216
   and executing batch jobs, 206–
     210
   PAUSE command and, 212
   REM command and, 210–211
BIN, 68
BIOS, 20
Blanks, and global identifiers, 72–
   73
Boot record, 25, 60
Booting, 6–10
   date entering and, 10
   from disk, 25–26
   FORMAT program and, 113
   time entering and, 12
Break function, 43
Byte, 2–3

Capital letter, 37
CapsLock key, 37
Characters, replacing, 185–189

CHKDSK, 130–132
Colons
   drive selection and, 27–28
   entering time and, 12
Color/Graphics Monitor Adapter, 5
COM, 45, 68
COMP command, 106, 125–129
COMMAND, 22–23
   command format and, 45
   command level and, 51–52
   control functions and, 44
   internal programs and, 50
   sending commands to, 40–41
Command Processor, *see* COM-
     MAND
Commands
   and batch processing, 203–220
   entering, 50
   error corrections, 41, 50–51
   file indentifier and, 47
   format, 45–50
   internal, *see* Internal commands
   suspension of, 43–44
   termination of, 46
   typing, 50–52
Communications equipment, 5–6
Concatenation
   copy command, 92–96
   date and time, 95
Control functions, 40–45
   and TYPE command, 68
COPY command, 83–102
   compared with DISKCOPY, 121–
     122
   concatenation, 92–96
   date and time, 95
   and destruction of data, 90